The
West Highland
Mallaig Extension
in BR days

Class K2 2-6-0 No. 61784 pauses at Arisaig with a Fort William-bound train on New Year's Day 1960.

(W.S. Sellar)

No. 37422 and a Mallaig-Fort William train between two of the tunnels on Beasdale Bank in June 1987.

The
West Highland
Mallaig Extension
in BR days

Tom Noble

Oxford Publishing Co.

Acknowledgements

It would be inappropriate to attempt to name all those who are due thanks for their assistance with this book, as inevitably, someone would be overlooked. I therefore extend a general, but no-less genuine, expression of gratitude to everyone who supplied photographs, provided information, answered my questions or simply pointed me in the right direction. All photographs are by the author, unless stated otherwise.

Title page: A Class 27 locomotive crosses Banavie Bridge with the 16.40 from Fort William on 2nd July 1975. Ben Nevis towers in the background.
(John Goss)

The unusual sight of a diesel locomotive working the green and cream steam set of coaches suggests that something has gone amiss. On this occasion, 28th May 1985, Black Five No. 44767 *George Stephenson* had been derailed at Mallaig Junction Yard, prior to working the 11.05 steam service from Fort William. Class 37 No. 37033 was substituted and the train is pictured nearing Loch Eil on the return trip. Most of the excursionists elected to travel despite the disappointment. However, the steam supplement charge was refunded.

The first actual failure of a steam locomotive occurred on 22nd August 1987, when No. 2005 suffered a holed boiler tube and a diesel took its place. Black Five No. 5305 stood in the following day.
(L.A. Nixon)

A FOULIS-OPC Railway Book

© 1989 T. Noble & Haynes Publishing Group

Published by:
Haynes Publishing Group
Sparkford, Near Yeovil, Somerset. BA22 7JJ

Haynes Publications Inc.
861 Lawrence Drive, Newbury Park, California 91320, USA.

Printed by J.H. Haynes & Co. Ltd.

British Library Cataloguing in Publication Data
Noble, Tom
The West Highland Mallaig extension.
1. Scotland. Highlands. Railways services: British
Rail, Scottish Region. West Highland line, history
I. Title
385'.09411'5

ISBN 0-86093-429-2

Library of Congress Catalog Card Number
89-84303

Foreword

by The Hon. W.H. McAlpine

I have always been particularly fond of the Mallaig Extension; not only because my great-grandfather built the line at the turn of the century, but also because, family considerations apart, it is simply a magnificent piece of railway.

I am delighted to travel on the line whenever I can and never fail to be impressed. It was particularly pleasing to be invited to unveil the name plate *Concrete Bob* on a Class 37 diesel locomotive, especially as the ceremony took place on the Glenfinnan Viaduct. The other side of the locomotive, as it were, had already been named Sir Robert McAlpine, at Fort William. At the time I wondered what my great-grandfather would have thought. The contract was a great struggle, at one stage looked disastrous and one of his sons was nearly killed on it. In addition, Concrete Bob was a nickname given to Sir Robert by his competitors laughing at his obsession with concrete. I came to the conclusion that he would have been surprised, but very proud of his two sided tribute.

The Extension is now not exactly as my great-grandfather constructed it. Station buildings, in particular, have fallen victim to changing economics. However, the major civil engineering features remain and Sir Robert would still recognise it as 'his' railway.

My love of the steam locomotive and my deeply-held conviction that the nation's railway heritage must be maintained for the benefit of future generations are both well-known. I am therefore particularly delighted that this book features strongly the steam renaissance of recent years, which has helped secure the future of the Mallaig Extension.

Totally individual, breathtakingly scenic, historically and socially significant . . . the Extension is all of these. More importantly it is a living working railway. Here's to the centenary in 2001!

The scene at the west end of Glenfinnan Viaduct on 14th October 1986, when W.H. (Bill) McAlpine formally named No. 37425 *Concrete Bob,* in honour of his great grandfather, builder of the Mallaig Extension. Earlier in the day, another ceremony was held at Fort William station, at which was unveiled the nameplate *Sir Robert McAlpine,* carried on the other side of the same locomotive! W.H. McAlpine (left) is pictured with the then ScotRail General Manager Jim Cornell, who presented him with a pair of replica nameplates.

Introduction

The line from Fort William to Mallaig has become something of legend. Acknowledged as unprofitable from the day it was born, it has survived the Beeching Era, which saw the demise of many routes with similar patterns of operation, and has hung onto life through a period of retrenchment and minimum investment. It has been rewarded in recent years with a fillip in the shape of regular steam-hauled excursions, which have opened up the delights of the Extension to thousands of visitors.

To many people, the railway west of Fort William seems as far removed in spirit from more southerly parts of the network as it is in reality. However, it would be wrong to confuse an undoubtedly more relaxed atmosphere with a casual approach to running a railway. It is simply that decades of being subjected to the vagaries of ferries at the west end of the route and main line trains at the other tended to nurture a pragmatic view of timetabling.

This is as it should be. The line was, after all, built for the benefit of the local population. It is its value to the community that has kept it alive, not its considerable appeal to the tourists who crowd its summer trains, welcome as they may be. The rail line is still a vital link, despite the growth in car ownership. Until January 1987, when a minibus began operating between Mallaig and Fort William, there was no bus service west of Corpach, apart from a small local operation around Morar and Mallaig. The road between Lochailort and Mallaig still has sections of single-track with passing places, although 1988 saw considerable improvements. However, thanks to the railway, children in the west could attend secondary school in Fort William and return home every evening. That may not sound impressive to an accountant in London but it matters a lot to a teenager in Arisaig. It is also just one small example of how the railway is the servant of the community.

This thread of social importance is woven throughout the origins of the Iron Road to the Isles. These go back to the 1880s, when politicians – and to a lesser extent landowners – began to acknowledge that, in parts of the Western Highlands, people were still leading a feudal existence, living hand-to-mouth on crofting and fishing. A Royal Commission was set up, under Lord Napier, which resulted in the Crofters Act of 1886. This fixed fair rents and gave crofters security of tenure, removing the threat of eviction at the whim of the landlord.

The Napier Commission was adamant that lack of transport facilities was stifling the development of the Western Highlands and Islands. Its report, published in 1884, said existing railheads of Oban and Strome Ferry were insufficient and recommended new railways. In 1888 the North British Railway, sensing a change in the political climate, gave its backing to a fresh bid to connect Lochaber by rail with Central Scotland. A previous grandiose scheme, called the Glasgow & North Western Railway, had failed to receive Parliamentary assent in 1883, when the Highland Railway was one of the main opponents.

By the end of the 1880s, however, opinion was on the side of the promoters of the West Highland Railway, and theirs was the bid that succeeded where others had failed. Unfortunately, they were denied total victory. The West Highland Railway, as originally conceived, would have struck out westward from Fort William to a terminus beyond Lochailort at Roshven, overlooking the Sound of Arisaig.

Here a harbour was to have been established to handle the herring catches, which the railway would have speedily conveyed to the markets of the south. This was a vital element of the proposal, as only the West Coast herring traffic offered any chance of making the line pay. It was with mixed emotions that the promoters learned in 1889 that the Parliamentary committee had approved the preamble to the main part of the Bill, linking Fort William with the North British Railway at Craigendoran, because the financial lifeline to the herring grounds had been deleted.

Feudalism had struck again. A Professor Blackburn, Emeritus Professor of Mathematics at Glasgow University, owned 60,000 acres which included the site of the pier at Roshven. His opposition, and that of other landowners, influenced the Parliamentary committee.

Matters could not be left at that. The West Highland Railway had been denied the prime reason for its existence – to serve the crofting and fishing communities of the hitherto undeveloped Western Highlands. There were men of influence in favour of the line, as well as opposed to it, and lobbying of a Government which still had the words of the Napier Commission ringing in its ears led to the establishment of a Government committee which recommend that Mallaig, on the Sound of Sleat, should become the railway's western terminus.

When the appropriate Bill came before Parliament, there was, of course, opposition. The Highland Railway was poised to extend its truncated Dingwall and Skye Railway from Strome Ferry to Kyle of Lochalsh and saw another railhead at Mallaig, 20 miles south, as a threat to its fish and mail traffic. The Highland could hardly complain about the element of subsidy, as its extension westward was being built with the help of £45,000 of Government money. However, the Highland soon saw the writing on the wall and withdrew its objections, saving both sides legal expense. And so it was that, only days before the first train from the south pulled into Fort William in August 1894, Parliament passed the West Highland Railway (Mallaig Extension) Act, which authorised construction from Banavie to a new harbour at Mallaig. The WHR was at last to get to the sea.

At least, it was in theory. In practice, another massive hurdle lay ahead. It had been realised that, however desirable the West Highland Extension may have been on social grounds, it was economically a non-starter. The Government Committee which proposed Mallaig suggested a £100,000 subsidy to the builders. Meanwhile, the North British Railway declined to proceed with construction without Government assistance. The West Highland Railway (Guarantee) Bill was therefore laid before Parliament. Without approval of this, the quite separate West Highland Railway (Mallaig Extension) Act of July 1894 was useless.

The Guarantee Bill became something of a political football. Politicians, who could not have identified Fort William on a map had their lives depended on it, hotly debated the Bill because of the principle it represented, and not the people. The Liberals did not approve of subsidising public transport; the Tories did. The people of Lochaber did not hide their feelings when, to their chagrin, the Guarantee Bill failed.

Fortunately, sense prevailed and when the Bill came up again in the 1896 session of Parliament it was passed. The Treasury undertook to guarantee shareholders a dividend of three per cent on £260,000 – less than half the total cost of the line – for 30 years and conferred a grant of £30,000 towards the £45,000 harbour at Mallaig. There were also rating benefits accruing from sympathetic assessment. It did not please some English MPs that the Government was doing so much to help Highlanders "who had never helped themselves".

On 21st January 1897, work began on the new railway at Corpach, with Lady Margaret Cameron of Lochiel cutting the first sod. Her husband, Cameron of Lochiel, had long been an enthusiastic supporter of the line. Construction got under way at several points along the route. Engineers were Simpson and Wilson and the contractors were Robert McAlpine and Sons, both of Glasgow. The line left the West Highland Railway's Banavie branch at what became Banavie Junction and writhed through a variety of terrain for almost 40 miles before reaching Mallaig. The first 11 1/2 miles were relatively easy, in that access was readily attainable from Loch Eil, although no fewer than 17 sea walls had to be provided between Corpach and Kinlocheil, to protect the line from the often stormy waters.

It was once the route turned towards Glenfinnan that difficulties arose. The hardness of local stone made it virtually unworkable, even if sufficient masons could have been recruited for such a remote location, which was unlikely. McAlpine was a proponent of the then relatively untried building material of mass concrete and he utilised this extensively on the Mallaig line, for viaducts, platforms and buildings. Such was his enthusiasm, he became known as Concrete Bob.

The builders took the line across glens and rivers on beautiful concrete viaducts; they floated it across peat bogs; they excavated 100 cuttings and they tunnelled through some of the hardest rock in Britain. Originally, two tunnels were envisaged. Eventually, they needed eleven. Bad weather and shortage of labour hindered progress. Despite this, the line was completed within the 5 1/2 year-period specified in the original Act and the opening to traffic was on 1st April 1901. The stations were Banavie, Corpach, Locheilside, Glenfinnan, Lochailort, Beasdale (a private station for Arisaig House but available to the public), Arisaig, Morar and Mallaig. Only Glenfinnan, Lochailort and Arisaig had passing loops. Signalling was by the Railway Signal Co. of Liverpool, which provided signal boxes of its own design, with Stevens-pattern frames.

The Mallaig Extension settled down to a traffic routine which lasted decades; serving the communities west of Fort William, conveying passengers bound for the islands steamers and transporting fish to the south, although not to the extent claimed by the line's promoters. Tourist activity in summer contrasted with the mundane remainder of the year.

The Second World War brought new loops and sidings, new traffic and new faces, as a naval repair yard was established at Corpach. A feature of the 1950s was the appearance of an observation car between Fort William and Mallaig, in the summer of 1956. One of the two "beaver tail" observation cars originally built for the "Coronation" expresses introduced by the LNER between London and Edinburgh in July 1937, was attached to the 10.24am from Fort William, returning on the 2.45pm from Mallaig. Sixteen first or second class passengers enjoyed armchair comfort and superb scenic views for an additional charge of 2s 6d (12 1/2p) per single journey.

For the 1957 season, the car was overhauled and redecorated, the seating capacity increased to 20 and a loudspeaker system installed, over which a conductor could give a running commentary. Each speaker could be switched off individually, depending on the whim of the nearest passenger. The supplementary charge remained at 2s 6d (12 1/2p) single.

In 1958, a similar vehicle operated between Glasgow and Fort William. A year later, the beaver tail cars were rebuilt, to improve visibility. The Extension vehicle was rostered for two return trips each weekday, which involved removing the observation car from the Glasgow-Mallaig train at Fort William and substituting the other vehicle at the opposite end. Plus, of course, a similar operation with the locomotives, all within the cramped confines of Fort William station! These distinctive vehicles were taken off in the early 1960s and not replaced, until a former departmental inspection saloon appeared in 1980. The beaver tail cars, which will always be associated with West Highland publicity of the period, have been preserved: No. 1719 at the Lochty Railway in Fife and No. 1729 at Steamtown, Carnforth.

The early 1960s were a time of trauma for the Mallaig Extension, and, indeed the West Highland line in general. There were alarming doubts about the entire route's future until January 1963, when British Railways and Scottish Pulp (Developments) Ltd announced a 22-year agreement under which a new pulp and paper mill at Corpach would receive raw materials, and despatch finished products, by rail. Lochaber heaved a sigh of relief. The Reshaping of British Railways proposals of 1963 involved discontinuing local stopping services between Fort William and Mallaig, thereby closing Banavie, Locheilside and Beasdale. Fortunately, the Minister of Transport refused consent. About the same time as the mill began to boost traffic, British Railways decided it was uneconomical to carry the fish from Mallaig. The merchants were given only a matter of days to arrange road alternatives and yet another aspect of the line's character and heritage vanished into history.

An aura of despondency could be detected around the Mallaig Extension by the start of the 1980s. The pulp mill ceased operating in October 1980, with a resultant loss of rail traffic, although the paper mill was retained. Some years earlier Ullapool had replaced Mallaig as the Stornoway ferry terminal. The Extension had taken on a moribund air and prophets of doom were rife.

A change of management approach and outlook throughout Scotland's railways and the introduction of steam-hauled excursions in 1984 brought new life to the Mallaig line. Always a basic railway, it was simplified further in 1987, with the single-manning of locomotives and the coming, in December of that year, of Radio Electronic Token Block signalling. This was the first application on the West Highland lines of the system pioneered on the Dingwall to Kyle of Lochalsh and Thurso/Wick routes. In the run-up to RETB, semaphore signals at passing loops were removed and the loop points converted to loco-operated. This is done by making the switch blades trailable; ie the train wheels push the blades over on leaving the loop while a pre-pressurised hydraulic ram restores the blades behind the departed train, in readiness for the next train.

A new signalbox, in traditional style, was built at Banavie, to act as the RETB signalling centre for the entire West Highland network and also to control the swing bridge over the Caledonian Canal. It took over from the original Banavie Swing Bridge box in June 1987 (following which the old box was quickly demolished) although some six months were to elapse before the new building first assumed an

RETB role. It was in December 1987 that the Mallaig line signalmen's last remaining traditional task – that of exchanging the brass tokens authorising a train to occupy a particular section – was taken over by new technology. Developments in microprocessors and mobile radio systems had allowed a new concept in signalling and communications. Each locomotive is fitted with a cab-mounted radio and microprocessor unit, and has a unique identity code. Authority to proceed into a block section is given on a display panel, by means of a coded data telegram transmitted from Banavie. This ensures that the message is accurate and is sent to the correct locomotive. Communications between Banavie and the locomotives, both electronic and speech, are recorded. The signalman is provided with solid state interlocking and associated visual display monitors on which are given the current state of the line.

Semaphore signals were retained at Annat, which became a gate box controlling two level crossings into the paper mill. Following the extension of RETB to the Glasgow line, Mallaig Junction box continued to control Fort William station and immediate area, the existing colour light and semaphore signals remaining in place. The box, however, was renamed Fort William to avoid confusion in transmitted messages.

The official opening of Banavie control centre was 19th May 1988, in a ceremony carried out by the then Minister of State for Transport, Mr David Mitchell. Two signalmen per shift are required to handle the entire West Highland lines traffic, replacing 16 signal boxes.

This has helped reduce the cost base of the routes, as well as giving greater flexibility of operation. Further savings are anticipated by the replacement of locomotive-hauled stock with Class 156 'Sprinter' diesel multiple units. At the end of 1988, this saving was being put at £600,000 per annum.

With costs reduced to the minimum, substantial renewal of basic assets and an optimistic assessment of the condition of such major civil engineering features as the Glenfinnan Viaduct, the chances of the Mallaig Extension celebrating its centenary in 2001 look brighter than ever.

The modern face of the West Highland Extension: 'Sprinter' unit No. 156450 stands at Mallaig on 25th January 1989, two days after the introduction of these sets throughout the West Highland rail network, replacing locomotive-hauled trains. Six sets were required for five diagrams, with the units being maintained at Haymarket depot, Edinburgh. This resulted in the introduction of a daily through service each way between Edinburgh and the West Highlands. The unit pictured here had been one of a pair forming the 07.03 departure from Edinburgh, the sets splitting at Crianlarich, with the other going to Oban. The last service of the day from Mallaig, departing at 18.15, formed the through working to Edinburgh, arrival being booked for 00.37. Note that No. 156450 is fitted with snowploughs, in common with all the sets working Provincial Sector's West Highland services.

The Way West A description of the line

Journeys on the Mallaig Extension begin and end at Fort William station, for there has never been a spur linking the Extension with the main line to the South. The present Fort William terminus is a 1975 replacement for the 1894 original, through which a ring road now runs. For the purposes of this volume, the Mallaig line is taken as beginning at Mallaig Junction, although this is not historically the case. At the opening of the West Highland line on 7th August 1894, Mallaig Junction was known as Banavie Junction, for a branch was to run some 1 3/4 miles to a station and pier on the Caledonian Canal.

This branch did not open for traffic until 1st June 1895, the delay being largely caused by difficulties in constructing the viaduct over the River Lochy. Cast iron cylinders had to be sunk for the founding of the masonry piers which carry the four 80ft spans. The decking is attached halfway up the main girders, instead of on top of them, as was the practice elsewhere on the West Highland Railway.

The Mallaig Extension proper began from a point on the Banavie branch which became Banavie Junction, the original junction of that name being termed Mallaig Junction. This shortened the Banavie branch to under half-a-mile. It offered a rail and water route to Inverness by connecting with canal steamers. By the summer of 1939 the service was one trip from Banavie Pier to Fort William on Mondays, Wednesdays and Fridays and one in the reverse direction on Tuesdays, Thursdays and Saturdays. The branch's last passenger train ran on 2nd September 1939, an event which was somewhat overshadowed by the territorial aspirations of a certain Herr Hitler. Freight services nominally continued into BR days, being withdrawn in August 1951.

Today, there is little trace of Banavie Junction, on the Blar Mhor, but the embankment of the branch is discernible on both sides of the A830 road. On the Mallaig line, milepost zero was at Banavie Junction, which means some two miles have to be added to milepost readings, in order to gauge the distance from the present Fort William station.

Banavie station is the first stop. The building was demolished some years ago, as it suffered badly from vandalism following de-staffing. The railway crosses the Caledonian Canal by means of a bow-truss bridge, the steelwork for which was by Alex Findlay and Co. of Motherwell. The bridge pivots from the east bank to allow the passage of vessels. Originally manually operated, it has been converted to electric power. Immediately north of Banavie bridge is a series of eight closely spaced canal locks known as Neptune's Staircase.

After being eased over the bridge, the train accelerates through a cutting to Corpach, once one of the two main construction camps for the line and the point which the Caledonian Canal enters Loch Linnhe. Today, its industrial significance lies in the Wiggins Teape paper mill, occupying 80 acres at Annat Point. This was built as a pulp and paper mill and began production in 1965.

It was laid out for rail transport and in its heyday 350 tons of logs per day arrived by train from a specially-established depot at Crianlarich Lower. These log trains, which ran once a day in each direction, were a familiar sight on the West Highland. They utilised reconstructions of flat wagons formerly in use on the "Condor" express freight between Gushetfaulds (Glasgow) and Hendon (London). The 50 conversions, carried out at Barassie railway workshops,

involved stripping the flat wagons of most of their fittings and building on end and centre panels to form two large compartments, with open girder sides.

The last timber train from Crianlarich ran on 9th June 1980, in anticipation of the closure of the pulp mill side of the operation that October, as a result of which British Rail lost traffic worth £500,000 a year. The relationship with the paper mill continued and it is now served by the Speedlink network. Incoming traffic includes china clay from Cornwall, for which there are 14 wagons in circuit, and wood pulp. This was imported through such ports as Methil, Grangemouth and Montrose, arriving at Corpach in OBA and OCA wagons. By 1987, much of the pulp required was being shipped to Corpach, with rail providing a back-up service.

In 1986, two striking black and white bogie bulk carriers appeared. These were Procor PBA vehicles which originally carried Tripolyphosphate for Proctor and Gamble. On becoming redundant, they were hired to CPC (UK) to transport starch powder between Manchester and Corpach. Oil for the plant's boilers comes from Grangemouth, in block trains of nine tank wagons. In the other direction, consignments of finished paper in VDA and VGA vans were sent via Speedlink to customers all over Britain, until a change in manufacturing policy in 1987 under which the plant produced reels instead of sheeted paper. Rail continued to be used for despatch, employing curtain-sided wagons.

The pulp and paper mill was built alongside the site of a naval repair yard, created in 1942/43 and for which two loops were provided. Some of the yard buildings remain to this day and one of the sidings can be traced. Farther west, on what was a golf course, 200 concrete houses were erected for the yard personnel and their families. A siding was put in to handle building materials for what became known as Annat village. In the mid-1960s the area was turned into a caravan park. To break the 16-mile stretch between Mallaig Junction and Glenfinnan, a freight-only loop was installed at Camus-na-ha, near Annat village, involving a new signal box which came into use on 15th November 1942. This closed from 21st June 1964, being replaced by Annat.

Industry is left behind as the train follows a winding but level course along Loch Eil, stopping, if requested, at the only new station built since the line's birth. Loch Eil Outward Bound is a basic but adequate halt constructed by young people from the adjacent adventure centre, under ScotRail supervision. It opened on 20th April 1985 with Sir Donald Cameron of Lochiel following a family tradition and doing the honours. At the same time, locomotive No. 37111 was named *Loch Eil Outward Bound*.

The next station is Locheilside, also a request stop, and then it is on to the head of the loch and the climb to one of the most dramatic structures on this or any other railway. The brakes go on as the train slows to 25 mph for the crossing of the magnificent Glenfinnan Viaduct. The statistics are as striking as the structure itself. A total of 21 arches, of the standard 50ft span, carry the line 100 feet above the valley floor, on a curve of 12 chains radius. It is 416 yards long and, like the line's other viaducts, is built of mass concrete. The cost of this masterpiece has been quoted at £18,904.

The magnificence of the viaduct is rivalled only by the

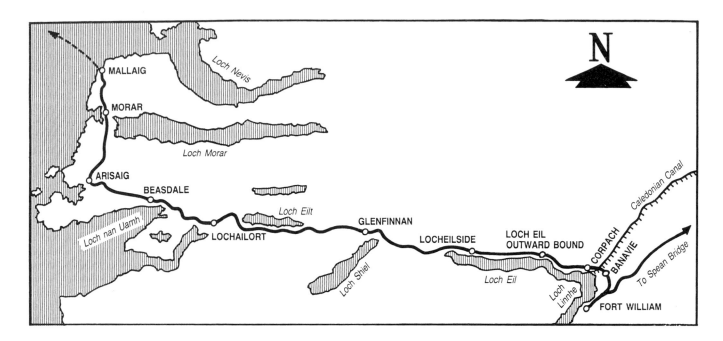

equally-impressive view it affords down Loch Shiel, flanked by walls of mountains. The foreground is dominated by the monument to Prince Charles Edward Stuart, who raised his standard at Glenfinnan when he landed from France to pursue his claim to the throne in what became the '45 Rebellion.

The speed restriction on the viaduct is followed by a stiff 1 in 45/50 climb up to Glenfinnan station, the first passing loop since Mallaig Junction, 16 miles away. West of Glenfinnan, the train follows the Shlatach Burn to the summit of the line, the watershed between Loch Shiel and Loch Eilt. Two of the Extension's eleven tunnels are encountered on the winding descent to Loch Eilt, along which road and railway take opposite shores.

At the western end of the loch, a causeway provides a superb photographic location, before the line suddenly swings north, crosses the foaming River Ailort on a concrete bridge, then turns westward again along Ailort Glen before reaching Lochailort station, now shorn of its passing loop, signal box and station building.

Lochailort has a significant place in the history of the line. It was here that the largest construction camp was established, housing at its peak 2000 men in huts of 40 bunks each. A schoolhouse was converted into an eight-bed hospital staffed by a doctor and two nurses. This was claimed to be Britain's first construction camp hospital. Provisions were supplied regularly by a Glasgow firm of merchants and a camp bakery ensured fresh bread. The navvies cooked their own meals on a communal hot plate – often using their brightly-polished shovels – and took their water from the burns.

There was rarely any shortage of water in the burns, which was one reason why, despite the remarkably progressive employment conditions, McAlpine found it difficult to retain labour. Many navvies had become accustomed to working in the growing Victorian towns and could not endure the West Highland weather and wilderness. The wages were good – up to fivepence an hour for a 55-hour week – and this helped the contractor retain a basic army of skilled labour, mostly Lowland Scots and

Irish, with Highlanders, Scandinavians and Gaelic-speaking fishermen from the Hebrides.

In the 1960s, a road was built from Lochailort to previously inaccessible areas of Moidart, eventually reaching Acharacle. This put paid to the once-daily mail boat which used to sail down Loch Shiel from Glenfinnan.

Beyond Lochailort station, McAlpine's men really earned their fivepence an hour. In the 8¼ miles from Lochailort to Arisaig, there are nine tunnels and several rock cuttings.

Initially, the line climbs to a picturesque white church, skirts Loch Dubh – the Black Loch – then bursts out of the trees to cross yet another concrete viaduct, at Loch nan Uamh – the Loch of the Caves. It was from here that Bonnie Prince Charlie fled to France in 1746, after the failure of the '45.

The train then begins the ascent of Beasdale Bank, 1½ miles of twisting, treacherous 1 in 48 gradient through heavily-wooded country, the rails often slippy from wet conditions. At the top is Beasdale station, unfortunately now derelict, but still a request stop.

The longest tunnel on the line (at 349 yards) is at Borrodale. It leads onto a viaduct which is yet another civil engineering feat. The landowner had insisted that the proposed viaduct over the Borrodale Burn should have its piers clad in granite, for appearances' sake. This was impossibly expensive so Concrete Bob opted for a single arch of 127 feet, which at the time was the largest single concrete span on any railway in the world. The castellated parapets were a sop to the landowner's aesthetic objections.

The next station – Arisaig – is the farthest west on British Rail. It was the first station on the West Highland lines to be converted to locomotive-operated points. This was done in early 1984 and in April of that year the signal box, which had been closed since the previous December, was reopened for the summer season, to allow trains to cross. When Arisaig box was open, electric token block working applied between Glenfinnan and Arisaig and one-train working regulations applied from Arisaig and Mallaig. When Arisaig was closed, there was one-train working from

Glenfinnan to Mallaig, the train staff for the Arisaig to Mallaig section being attached to the Glenfinnan – Arisaig token. This, of course, was superseded by radio signalling at the end of 1987.

The departure from Arisaig allows views over Loch nan Ceall to the islands beyond. The farthest-west point on the rail map of Britain is reached near Kinloid then the route is across Keppoch Moss to the shining sands of Morar, over the river by means of Morar Viaduct and on to Morar station. The familiar ritual of the train crew opening and closing the gates of the level crossing over the main road to Mallaig has now disappeared. Amid much local controversy, the crossing was converted to automatic open operation from 26th May 1985.

Five weeks later an incident occurred which did nothing to allay the villagers' misgiving about the lack of a barrier crossing. A car collided with a train. Not just any train, but the Royal train! A hired car driven by an American tourist met locomotive No. 37011 on the crossing as it and No. 37027 *Loch Eil* were hauling the fortunately empty stock back south, having transported the Prince and Princess of Wales to Mallaig for a visit to the Western Isles. No-one was hurt, there was very little damage and the tourist subsequently claimed he thought that a flashing red light meant *be prepared* to stop!

The issue flared up again in July 1986 when the warning system malfunctioned on several occasions, failing to switch off after the passage of a train. In one instance it sounded for 15 hours. Unfortunately, it was the same weekend as the Lockington train crash, which claimed the lives of nine people and involved a similar type of crossing.

At Mallaig, the station building – in an architectural style known as 'vernacular revival' – has been upgraded in recent years. On the signalling side, Mallaig box was taken out as a block post in March 1982 and the semaphore signals were cut down. The signal box remains, in order that train crews can operate the points.

Further contraction appeared likely in 1983, when it was announced that the train crew base was to be closed from October of that year, with the men being made redundant or transferred. Stock would have been worked empty to Mallaig to begin the day's service, returning empty to Fort William late at night. Not surprisingly, the proposal encountered considerable resistance which led to first a temporary reprieve then, in February 1984, abandonment. At the time, five drivers, five driver's assistants and three guards were based at Mallaig.

Like the railway, the town of Mallaig is something of a survivor. Not only has it seen its importance as a ferry port reduced, it has had to cope with the unthinkable, in the shape of a ban on herring fishing. For too long, the fish were scooped from the sea like there was no tomorrow . . . but suddenly, tomorrow really did come. To conserve stocks, a ban was imposed on North Sea herring fishing in 1977, followed in 1978 by a similar restriction off the West Coast of Scotland. Mallaig, once Europe's premier herring port, had to turn to other catches, such as shellfish, for the West Coast ban lasted until 1981 and North Sea restrictions were not relaxed until 1983. By 1987, Mallaig was Britain's leading prawn port, with annual landings amounting to more than £7m.

All of which was academic as far as the railway was concerned, for BR withdrew from fish traffic about 1965, apart from salmon which travelled, packed in ice-filled boxes, in the guard's van of passenger trains.

At the time of writing, Mallaig is undergoing a process of rejuvenation. Some £8m of EEC, Scottish Development Agency and Scottish Development Department money is being spent on the village (population 1,200). Of this, £3.5m has gone on a new two-mile access road, coming between the railway and the shore, which was opened on 29th July 1988. Another £2.5m is being used to upgrade the local secondary school to six-year status, which will mean the end of senior pupils travelling (often by train) to Lochaber High School in Fort William. Improvements to leisure and commercial facilities are also being carried out.

Several reminders of the railway's past have recently disappeared. In 1987, the old locomotive shed was an early victim of the road-building scheme. Also that year, the screen wall behind the station platform was demolished. In 1988, the former railway dormitory had to be knocked down, following a fire in June. This building, used mainly by the men who handled the railway fish traffic, had been empty for many years and in August 1984 was sold for a nominal £1 to house a heritage museum, a project which appears to have made little progress in the intervening period.

A newcomer for the 1989 season: Black Five No. 44871 tackles Beasdale Bank on 1st June 1989 with the 10.35 service from Fort William. This was the last standard gauge steam locomotive to work in BR service in August 1968 and is now owned by an all-Scottish consortium.

Right: No. 37112 has slightly more than half a mile of its journey left as it comes off the Extension at Mallaig Junction with the 15.50 eastbound service on 4th July 1985. The stock, which came north on the 05.50 from Glasgow, will be reunited with the Euston sleepers and leave as the 17.40 departure from Fort William. The line on the left of the picture serves an oil distribution depot.

Mallaig Junction

Below: A different view of Mallaig Junction, with the line to Glasgow in the foreground. The date is 31st August 1987 and No. 37413 *Loch Eil Outward Bound* is pictured taking the Mallaig route with the 10.05 from Fort William. The wooden platforms on either side of the signal box were utilised by the signalman when collecting the single line token from the train crews. Once RETB was extended to the main line to Craigendoran, the signal box was renamed Fort William and continued to control the station and approaches.

Right: The location is Lochyside, on the outskirts of Fort William, and No. 37026 *Loch Awe* and the 07.00 from Mallaig are seen passing Banavie 'down' distant signal, on 8th August 1983. The locomotive and crew were diagrammed to work the 09.19 Fort William – Glasgow. The Mallaig men returned with the 06.00 ex-Glasgow, the booked changeover being Spean Bridge.

Below: Ben Nevis, gratifyingly free of cloud, dominates the background, as No. 37412 and the 16.05 Fort William – Mallaig of 1st August 1986 approach the level crossing over the Caol road at Banavie, which was commissioned in February 1983. The signal beyond the train is at the site of the former Banavie Junction.

Right: The origins of this private house – photographed in 1983 – are readily apparent. It was formerly Banavie Pier station, terminus of the branch linking the West Highland Railway with the Caledonian Canal. The pier was considerably higher than the station and wagons were back-shunted up a gradient of 1 in 24 to the canal bank.

Banavie

Right: The RETB control centre at Banavie was officially opened by the then Minister of State for Transport, Mr David Mitchell, on 19th May 1988. One of the two operators controlling the entire West Highland network is pictured at work, with the canal bridge visible in the background.

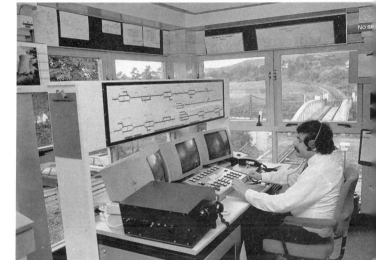

Below: The east end of Banavie station on 27th May 1985, with No. 37191 *International Youth Year 1985* leaving with the 06.50 from Mallaig. This locomotive was named on 21st January of that year and carried its plates only until the following November.

Above: The railway bridge over the Caledonian Canal at Banavie pivots from the east bank to allow the passage of small vessels. For many years, the canal has been used chiefly by pleasure craft and fishing boats wishing to avoid the long – and sometimes hazardous – journey around the north of Scotland. In this May 1987 picture, the bridge has opened in order that the *Grenaa Star* of Grimsby can begin the 60 mile voyage to Clachnaharry, near Inverness – the other end of the canal.

Right: This distinctive signal controlled the approach to Banavie Swing Bridge from the west and was one of the casualties of the abolition of semaphores in June 1987. After being cut down, the post lay by the trackside for quite some time. The locomotive is No. 37405 *Strathclyde Region,* at the head of a Mallaig-bound train.

Above: The hills in the background carry a generous dusting of late snow as No. 37402 *Oor Wullie* eases the 16.05 from Fort William across Banavie bridge on 22nd May 1986. The locomotive will be opened up for the short climb to Corpach as soon as the two vintage vehicles on the rear clear the steelwork. These are being used for private rail-based luxury holidays. The post on the right once carried a sign which read "speed 40 miles".

Over the Bridge

Left: Class K1 2-6-0 No. 62034 takes the 10.05 Glasgow-Mallaig over the canal at Banavie on 17th July 1961.
(Douglas Hume)

Banavie bridge, from the north side, on 23rd June 1986. The signalman exchanges tokens with the crew of No. 37404 *Ben Cruachan* as it and the 06.50 from Mallaig thud across.

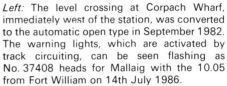
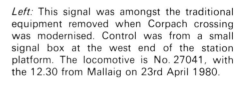

Corpach

Left: The level crossing at Corpach Wharf, immediately west of the station, was converted to the automatic open type in September 1982. The warning lights, which are activated by track circuiting, can be seen flashing as No. 37408 heads for Mallaig with the 10.05 from Fort William on 14th July 1986.

Left: This signal was amongst the traditional equipment removed when Corpach crossing was modernised. Control was from a small signal box at the west end of the station platform. The locomotive is No. 27041, with the 12.30 from Mallaig on 23rd April 1980.

Below: No. 37022 accelerates away from Corpach with the 16.30 Fort William-Mallaig in August 1983. The last coach has just passed the Annat 'down' distant signal, which was replaced by a reflectorised distant board in April 1985. At this point, the line is bordering Loch Linnhe.

Above: Class 20 No. 20114 ambles past Corpach with a trip working from Mallaig Junction Yard to the Wiggins Teape paper mill. On this August day in 1983, the load is china clay in the first three wagons and wood pulp. Much of the factory's raw material comes in by rail, although by 1987 pulp was also being shipped to Corpach.

Right: A Class 37/4, No. 37412 heads west on the approach to Annat signal box on 1st August 1986. The locomotive is passing a siding which recalls the loops installed in 1942 as part of the naval repair yard constructed at Annat. Examination of the undergrowth behind the photographer revealed that the siding quickly became lightweight track which ended in a brick building, used for commercial purposes. The line could have served an auction market but appeared not to have carried a train in many a long year. Not surprisingly, the connection has since been taken out.

Above: The 06.50 from Mallaig, powered by the inevitable Class 37/4, approaches Annat signal box on 20th May 1987. Annat dates from June 1964, when it replaced Camus-na-ha following the setting-up of the pulp mill. The pitched roof is a very recent acquisition– the original was flat – and some of the steps have metal plates lettered LMS. It ceased to be a block post with the introduction of RETB but remained as a gate box, controlling two level crossings.

Above: Former BR Class 08 No. 08077 propels empty vans into the despatch bay of the Corpach paper mill on 5th March 1985. Apart from the lack of numbers and logos, the locomotive looks much as it did before BR sold it to Wiggins Teape in 1978.

Above: Overpowering? Nos 37409 and 20213, in what seems an excessive use of tractive effort, take two empty vans into the Corpach paper mill sidings on 14th July 1986. In truth, the Class 20 was being returned to Eastfield depot on the 10.20 Corpach-Mossend Speedlink and was coupled to No.37409 in advance of this.

Right: Around April 1985, reflectorised distant boards replaced distant signals all over the West Highland lines. This is Annat up distant post in May 1985, with its usurper alongside. The bridge gives access to the caravan park on the site of the wartime Annat village. Camus-na-ha loop was on the stretch of line behind the photographer.

Below: It took 84 years for the Mallaig Extension to see its first additional station. It was on 20th April 1985 that Loch Eil Outward Bound opened, a sleeper platform built under ScotRail supervision by young people from the adventure centre. A waiting shelter was added in July 1988. No. 37014 is seen approaching on 21st May 1985, with the 06.50 from Mallaig. Milepost $4^{1}/_{4}$ on the left marks the distance from the site of Banavie Junction, original starting point of the Extension.

Above: Locheilside, Banavie and Lochailort station buildings experienced a similar pattern of destaffing, vandalism and demolition. This is Locheilside in June 1968, derelict and doing nothing to enhance the line's image.
(J.L. Stevenson)

Above: Locheilside in July 1986. Surely this is not what is meant by the term "open station"?

Along Loch Eil

Above: For some years, the only regular freight traffic west of Corpach has been diesel fuel from Grangemouth to Mallaig, for use by ferries and fishing vessels. It was conveyed attached to passenger trains, usually the late afternoon service from Fort William. This is the train featured in this picture, taken near Locheilside on 23rd June 1986. The locomotive is No. 37408.

Left: The morning of 1st September 1987 finds No. 37407 *Loch Long* hauling a civil engineering train eastwards out of Glenfinnan, having been held at the station to cross the 10.05 from Fort William.

Glenfinnan

Below: A classic view of the Glenfinnan Viaduct, highlighting its 12-chain radius curve. Locomotive No. 27006 will doubtless be doing no more than 25 mph as it heads west with a Mallaig train on 1st July 1974. This particular Class 27 had only 18 months of working life ahead of it, being withdrawn in January 1976 following fire damage. *(John Goss)*

Above: Few travellers can fail to be impresssed by the mass concrete Glenfinnan Viaduct and the panoramic views down Loch Shiel which it provides. Its 416 yard length makes even a Class 37 locomotive and five coaches appear insignificant. The east abutment (left of picture) and six of the piers are founded on rock; the remainder rest on boulders and compacted gravel. Piers 8 and 13 are considerably thicker than the rest. An apocryphal story is told of a horse and cart falling into one of the hollow piers during the viaduct's construction and being entombed there to this day.

Right: On 31st May 1972, Sulzer-engined Type 2 No. 5352 picks up speed after the 25 mph restriction over Glenfinnan Viaduct and continues its progress eastward with the 14.05 from Mallaig. The locomotive illustrates an early rail blue livery, in which the cab side windows did not have yellow surrounds. No. 5352 later became No. 27006.
(John Cooper-Smith)

Off into the evening sun. No. 37175 and the two-coach 21.05 Fort William – Mallaig rumble across Lochy Viaduct on 29th June 1984. Next morning, this locomotive failed at Locheilside whilst working the 06.50 from Mallaig.

Above: On 4th August 1986, Class 20 No. 20048 approaches Corpach level crossing with a trip working of vans from the nearby paper mill, bound for Mallaig Junction Yard. From there a Class 37 will take them south, as the 10.20 Corpach – Mossend Speedlink. The paper mill can be seen on the left.

Right: Question: What do you do when the locomotive on the early morning train from Mallaig expires at Lochailort and the nearest replacement is 25 miles away at Fort William? Answer: Send the nearest replacement! Which is why the 06.50 from Mallaig of 4th August 1986 is well behind time as it is hauled past Lochyside, on the outskirts of Fort William, by No. 37425 which was despatched to rescue failed No. 37404 *Ben Cruachan.* Note how the orange stripe on No. 37425 continues down the windscreen pillars and across the rear of the bonnet, a feature which it lost when spruced up for its naming ceremony in October 1986.

Top left: The crew prepare for a token exchange as Class 27 No. 27019 eases across Banavie swing bridge, over the Caledonian Canal, with the 07.00 Mallaig – Fort William on 20th June 1977. The bridge was repainted yellowish-brown in mid-1985.

Bottom left: Banavie signal boxes, old and new, on 22nd June 1986. As well as the canal bridge, the original box controlled the approach to a level crossing situated between it and the station. This was superseded in February 1983 by a half-barrier crossing over a new road into Caol. The new signal box, construction of which was well under way at the time of this photograph, is the control centre for Radio Electronic Token Block signalling. At least it looks like a signal box!

Above: No. D6129, one of the North British Locomotive Co. Type 2 locomotives re-engined in 1967, hauls an 'up' train past Loch Eil in April of that year. Very few Class 29s received this blue livery.
(Derek Cross/Colour-Rail)

Above: Against a dramatic but threatening sky, No. 37039 accelerates away from Loch Eil Outward Bound station with the 06.50 Mallaig-Fort William on 28th May 1985.

BRCW Type 2 (later Class 27) No. D5359 in front of the turntable at Mallaig shed, in August 1964. *(B.E. Timmins/Colour Rail)*

Above: On a line which abounds with spectacular features, one of the highlights must be the viaduct at Loch nan Uamh. In either direction, trains burst out of cuttings or tunnels and onto this eight-arch viaduct. An unusual sight on 31st May 1985 was No. 37188 *Jimmy Shand* and the Fison's weedkilling train, which was on its annual visit. The train is heading back to Fort William, which it left at 05.25 that morning, and has the journey to Oban ahead of it before ending its working day at Dumbarton at 22.35. The locomotive has strong West Highland connections, having been named at Oban on 10th May 1985.

Above: Mirrored in Loch Eilt, No. 44932 heads west with a service train in September 1986.

Above: The InterCity executive saloon, off the West Highlander excursion from London, was pressed into service on 28th June 1987 for the steam-hauled section of the trip. It is the vehicle immediately behind No. 5305.

Above: The maximum number of coaches a locomotive can easily run round at Mallaig is six. That was the load for No. 37409 on 21st June 1986, seen with the 14.05 from Fort William near its journey's end.

Below: Eastfield-based Class K2 2-6-0 No. 61794 *Loch Oich* simmers in the sunshine outside Mallaig shed in September 1959. *Loch Oich* had two years of life ahead of it; the depot not much more. The building became a fish box store and the roofless shell survived until 1987.
(J.J. Davis/Colour Rail)

Left: An observation saloon reappeared on the Mallaig Extension in the summer of 1980 when former LNER saloon DE 902260, modified to provide random seating for up to 30 passengers, was attached to the 13.15 from Fort William and 16.03 return. The single journey supplement of 75p provided a reserved seat, souvenir ticket and conductor commentary. The Thompson-designed saloon, built in 1945, was named *Lochaber* at Fort William on 6th June 1980. *Lochaber,* which was numbered Sc1999, was also employed the following year and is seen leaving Mallaig on 3rd June 1981. The train is the 16.10 departure, with No. 37114 in charge.

Left: Sunday 14th July 1985 finds No. 37178 stabled at Glenfinnan. The Stevens-type ground shunt signal in the foreground was a product of the Railway Signal Co. and had the letters NBR on the lamp housing cover and green spectacle plate arm. It was removed, along with the semaphore signals, in early 1986, when locomotive-operated points were installed.

Below: Beasdale Bank, initially 1^1/$_2$ miles of 1 in 48, is reputed to be the most treacherous gradient on the entire West Highland line, a title for which there is no shortage of contenders. No. 44932 was captured in full flight on Beasdale, on 7th September 1986.
(John Cooper-Smith)

Above: A fine example of a semaphore signal holds a Class 37 at Glenfinnan in September 1983. The train is the 16.30 from Fort William, waiting to meet the 16.10 from Mallaig. To save money, Mallaig line stations were built with sleeper crossings, such as this one, instead of footbridges. Glenfinnan's semaphores were removed in the Spring of 1986.

Right: The Mallaig Extension has seen a variety of 2-6-0 locomotives. Towards the end of steam it played host to the BR Standard Class 4MT No. 76001, which is seen leaving Glenfinnan with a westbound afternoon train in the summer of 1960.
(Gavin Morrison)

Left: A Scottish Railway Preservation Society railtour, behind a Class 25 locomotive, photographed on the Glenfinnan Viaduct on 5th August 1978. The fifth vehicle is the Society's teak-bodied LNER buffet, which has put in sterling railtour service. The headboard? Probably another SRPS idiosyncrasy.
(W.S. Sellar)

Below: The North British Locomotive Company's Type 2 No. D6124 – one of the handful of Class 29s which received blue livery, poses at Glenfinnan with a train from Mallaig in June 1968.
(J.L. Stevenson)

Below: Camping coaches were once a feature of West Highland stations, notably Rannoch, Spean Bridge, Glenfinnan, Arisaig and Morar. Their origins were as diverse as their styles. Towards the end, this clerestory vehicle could be found at Glenfinnan, designated *Pullman Camping Coach No. 51.* It was photographed on 6th June 1968. The Ford Anglia alongside is an equally interesting exercise in design, of a different sort!
(J.L Stevenson)

Contrasts in leaving Glenfinnan

Right: One of the reasons why the operating authorities at Fort William preferred a Class 20 for shunting and tripping duties was that it could be pressed into passenger service on the Extension when a Class 37 was not available, although it could not provide train heating. That was the situation on 6th August 1986, when No. 20048 was caught leaving Glenfinnan with the 16.05 to Mallaig. (However, every silver lining has a cloud; in this case, the two comedians in the first coach.)

Below. There are no objections to the waving arm in this shot, as it belongs to the driver of Class K1 2-6-0 No. 62011. His locomotive is pulling away from Glenfinnan with the 9.55 am Fort William-Mallaig on 17th July 1961. A rebuilt beaver tail observation car is on the rear. *(Douglas Hume)*

Top right: The last Class 27 in revenue-earning service was No. 27008, withdrawn on 18th August 1987. Long before the class became a threatened species, No. 27008 was photographed coasting down to Lock Eilt from the summit of the line with a Mallaig-bound train on 2nd July 1975.
(John Goss)

Bottom right: No. 37423 and the 14.05 Fort William-Mallaig skirt Loch Eilt on 18th August 1987 – the day the locomotive in the previous picture was withdrawn!

Above: Snow has rarely presented problems on the Extension. In fact, at its western extremity, the climate can be remarkably mild, even in the depths of winter. Photographs of the line depicting snow in any amount therefore seem to be rare. In this 15th February 1979 view, No. 27011 and the morning train from Fort William are threading through the reverse curves west of Glenfinnan, near the summit of the line.
(Brian Morrison)

Right: Same spot; different season; different motive power. No. 37184 heads west with the 14.05 from Fort William on a sunny 30th June 1984.

Left: Island-dotted Loch Eilt stretches eastward in the background as No. 27019 and the 10.03 Glasgow–Mallaig leave one of the causeways at the loch's western end on 1st July 1974. *(John Goss)*

Right: At the western end of Loch Eilt, the line swings north for a short distance and runs alongside the River Ailort, as it flows into the loch. This is the location in this striking study of No. 37012 *Loch Rannoch* and the 10.05 Fort William–Mallaig seen on 31st May 1985. *(L.A. Nixon)*

Below: No. 27109 and the 14.05 from Mallaig amid the hills east of Lochailort on 2nd July 1975. This train ran to Glasgow Queen Street (arrive 20.29) and Edinburgh (arrive 23.09), but by changing at Glasgow, passengers could be in the Capital by 21.43! *(John Goss)*

Above: The sun glints off the windscreen of No. 37051 as it approaches Lochailort with the 16.30 from Fort William on 8th August 1983. Lochailort was the location of one of the two main construction camps for the line. The area resounded to the tramp of heavy boots again during World War Two, when it was a Commando training ground. As a result, the station handled numerous troop trains. Glenfinnan was similarly involved.

Lochailort

Left: Of the intermediate stations between Fort William and Mallaig, only Glenfinnan, Lochailort and Arisaig were built with passing loops. Lochailort was the first to lose this facility; however this had not yet happened by 17th July 1961 when K1 class 2-6-0 No. 62012 was pictured arriving with the 1.00 pm from Mallaig.
(Douglas Hume)

Above: Lochailort station building on 3rd June 1983. The loop has gone, the building is derelict. The last discernible date of painting is 1st June 1961. Shortly after this picture was taken, the demolition squad moved in.

Above: The austere brick signal box at Lochailort closed in 1966. When photographed in June 1983, it was a bothy and the steps and railings had recently been painted. It was demolished in early 1986.

Above: Lochailort on 21st September 1983. The foundations are being prepared for the "bus shelter" which replaced the station building.

Right: In the summer of 1977, mail is unloaded from the 10.30 Fort William-Mallaig, as the train pauses at Lochailort, which serves as a railhead for the Moidart peninsula.

Above: One of Fort William shed's five Class K1 2-6-0s, No. 62031, near Lochailort with a westbound goods in July 1961, when the end of steam on the Extension was only months away. Fort William's K1s – Nos 62011/12/31/34/52 – were then either dumped at Bo'ness or transferred to the North Eastern Region. *(Douglas Hume)*

Left: Standard Class 4MT 2-6-0 No. 76001, which Fort William shed had acquired from Motherwell for the summer of 1960, was still around the following year. As the West Highland perpetuated the North British Railway practice of coupling the pilot locomotive inside, K1 class No. 62052 must be taken as the train engine in this view of the two locomotives heading the 5.10 am Glasgow-Mallaig out of Lochailort, in July 1961. *(Douglas Hume)*

Class K1 2-6-0 No. 62034 makes a stylish assault on the gradients above Lochailort with an afternoon train from Fort William. The shedcode plate reads 65J, which was Fort William between 1955 and 1960. Previously, it had been 63D and from 1960 until closure in 1962, Fort William shed was coded 63B.
(W.J.V. Anderson)

Left: This viaduct, of standard mass concrete construction, lies amid heavily wooded scenery, before the line reaches the better-known structure at Loch nan Uamh. Pictured on 28th May 1985 are No. 37037 and the 14.05 from Fort William.

Below: The inspection vehicle acting as an observation saloon is prominent in this view of the 10.05 from Fort William crossing Loch nan Uamh Viaduct on 28th May 1984, the day a steam locomotive set the Extension alight. Evidence of this can be seen on the hillside.

Top left: A supremely evocative photograph of Class K2 2-6-0 No. 61791 *Loch Laggan* hard at work near Lochailort with a Fort William-Mallaig goods in June 1950. The sheer variety of vehicles in this lengthy train contrasts sharply with the moribund impression given off by the Mallaig Extension in more recent times. (*W.J.V. Anderson*)

Bottom left: In scenery such as this, the leisurely progress of the trains can be forgiven. Class 37 No. 37027 *Loch Eil* and the 12.20 Mallaig-Fort William swing round the east end of Loch Dubh – the Black Loch – on 21st May 1985. The next call will be at Lochailort.

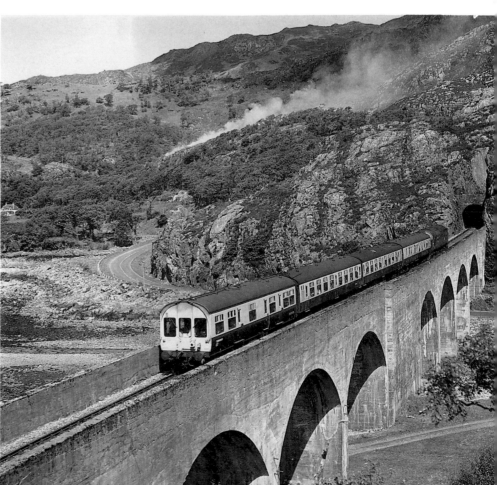

Beasdale

Right: Beasdale was originally a private station for Arisaig House which is why it differs in design from other Extension station buildings, although sharing concrete as the method of construction. It also shared the fate of some of the others and by June 1983 was a mere shell. Although private, Beasdale was available to the public from the date of opening.

Right: In August 1986, the short siding at Beasdale was still in place, as was the equipment allowing access. This was something of a museum piece, consisting of a Railway Signal Co. lever frame, reading LSW 1898 on one side and LSW 1900 on the other. The levers were unlocked by an equally interesting Stevens tablet instrument, at the base of which a plate proclaimed: "British Railways Historical Relic claimed through the stores controller Derby. Enquiries to 01-642 5462". A year later, this relic was noted removed. The pointwork appeared to be LNER, with the locking bar mechanism carrying the date 1939. Catch points were provided in the siding, interconnected with the main line points.

Below: Beasdale and its siding on 27th July 1987, with No. 37406 *The Saltire Society* rattling through on the 10.05 ex-Fort William. The siding was removed early in 1988.

Above: No. 37424 drifts down the bank towards Beasdale with the 12.20 from Mallaig on 8th August 1986. The ETH-fitted Class 37/4s established a firm grip on West Highland services in October 1985, taking over from the 37/0s which in turn had displaced the 27s.

Right: At the date of photographing, which was 28th May 1985, Class 37 No. 37037 represented the typical West Highland line locomotive of the time. Dual braked, boiler fitted, snowploughs all year round, Eastfield terrier motif and that other trademark of its home depot – black marker light panels. The location is the summit west of Borrodale and the train is the 12.20 Mallaig-Fort William.

Arisaig

Right: Towards the end of 1983 the signal arms at Arisaig were removed and the loop secured out of use, prior to the installation of loco-operated points. This scene, with No. 37051, taken at the west end, has therefore passed into history.

Below: The interior of Arisaig signal box, while it was still in operation. The frame was of the Stevens pattern.

Below: Apart from the signalling alterations, Arisaig has changed little since Class K1 locomotives Nos 62031 and 62012 were recorded on the 5.45 am from Glasgow to Mallaig on 21st July 1958. It seems incongruous that the farthest west station in Britain was once the preserve of the London & North Eastern Railway! *(W.A.C Smith)*

Above: On 1st June 1985, Nos 37111 *Loch Eil Outward Bound* and 37081 *Loch Long* leave Arisaig with SLOA's "West Highlander" railtour. Running round the nine vehicles involved some complicated shunting at Mallaig.
(L.A. Nixon)

Below: Keppoch Moss, a bog across which the builders had to float the line on brushwood, is the location of this shot of No. 37088 and the 10.05 from Fort William, also on 1st June 1985.
(L.A. Nixon)

Above: The River Morar, favourite of salmon fishermen, spills out of Loch Morar, Scotland's deepest loch, under another of Concrete Bob's creations. On 1st July 1974, No. 27006 crosses the Morar Viaduct with the 14.05 Mallaig-Glasgow/Edinburgh.
(John Goss)

Morar

Left: No. 37051 and the 16.30 Fort William-Mallaig approach Morar on 3rd June 1981, passing the fixed distant signal which applied to the gated crossing over the A830 road. The finial was removed before the signal was abolished in May 1985. The marker lights positioned at the edges of the former headcode boxes gave the Class 37s a strange "cross-eyed" appearance.

The saga of Morar level crossing

Left: An economy drive resulted in the level crossing gates at Morar being opened and closed by train crews, a practice which lasted for many years. Six minutes were once allowed for this operation. In this June 1977 picture, the guard of the 13.00 from Mallaig is closing the gate behind his train. A small signal box – similar to the installation which once stood at Corpach – was situated at the platform end, next to the faraway gate. After closure, the wooden structure survived until at least late 1973. Morar station building, which was derelict for some time, became a pottery in recent years and latterly a shop.

The south end of Morar crossing on 1st July 1974 finds No. 27019 easing through with the 12.09 Mallaig – Fort William. This train was a local service running from 27th May until 30th September.
(John Goss)

Left: The gated crossing at Morar was replaced by an automatic open system from 26th May 1985. A few days earlier, this picture was taken of the installation work. (The notice on the left always seemed to be stating the obvious, but no doubt some warning was required.) Local people who were opposed to an open crossing continued to be critical, although ScotRail had to contend with motorists parking on the crossing.

Left and below: Rarely has the road sign for a level crossing been as appropriate as the one at Morar. A steam locomotive *does* cross this road – and a 4-6-0 at that! Just to prove it, Black Five No. 5407 and the 13.35 from Mallaig are pictured at the crossing on 8th September 1985. The picture was taken from a convenient viewpoint hill, the path to which was being reconstructed. Was the original track worn out by steam photographers?

Above: Non-standard motive power in the shape of No.20148 hauls a Mallaig – Fort William train towards Morar on 3rd June 1983. The signal was a fixed distant protecting the level crossing. *(L.A. Nixon)*

Morar to Mallaig

Right: No.37027 *Loch Eil* was repainted in large logo livery at Eastfield depot in April 1985. It had therefore been sporting this appearance for only a matter of weeks when it was photographed on 21st May 1985 near Mallaig with the 14.05 from Fort William, the two coaches of which seem a derisory load for a Class 37. The second vehicle has just cleared the Mallaig reflectorised distant board.

Above: In 1984/85, almost £2m was spent on developing Mallaig harbour, including the construction of a breakwater to give extra sheltered berthing for fishing vessels. The work resulted in a minor boost for the railway, as some steel came in by train. On 31st May 1985, for instance, the 14.05 from Fort William had bolster wagons, loaded with steel plate, attached to the rear. This unusual combination was captured on film as it left Morar, behind No. 37012 *Loch Rannoch.*
(L.A. Nixon)

Top right: From May 1985, the Fort William – London sleeper ran on Sundays instead of Saturdays, with the 17.40 Saturday departure from Fort William terminating in Glasgow. The entire stock for this train could therefore be employed on the 14.05 Fort William – Mallaig and 15.50 Mallaig – Glasgow, as no remarshalling was required at Fort William once the 15.50 arrived. On Saturday 21st June 1986, No. 37409 takes the 15.50 out of sun-drenched Mallaig. The West Highland Hotel in the background, incidentally, was once called the Station Hotel.

Bottom right: Across the Sound of Sleat, the Isle of Skye beckons as No. 37012 *Loch Rannoch* and the 15.50 to Fort William head away from Mallaig on 31st May 1985. The new road to Mallaig now occupies the area on the left.
(L.A. Nixon)

Steam at Mallaig

Above: Standard Class 4MT 2-6-0 No. 76001 shunts stock at Mallaig on 13th August 1960, prior to its next departure. The vehicle on the left of the picture is of interest in that it appears to have opening end doors and a drop-down flap above the buffers, recalling a short-lived Motorail service between here and Fort William, aimed at drivers who baulked at the tortuous A830. More than 25 years later, much of the route was still inadequate, particularly in view of the fish traffic gifted to the road industry by British Railways. The building visible behind the coach is a former railway dormitory, demolished in 1988.
(Gavin Morrison)

Above: Class K1/1 2-6-0 No. 61997 *MacCailin Mor* receives attention at Mallaig shed on 8th September 1959. The locomotive had stalled climbing Beasdale Bank with the morning train from Fort William. The contents of the smokebox may have been a contributory factor! *MacCailin Mor*, LNER No. 3445, was originally a Class K4 until Edward Thompson rebuilt it with two cylinders in 1946, as part of a developing standardisation policy.
(J.J. Davis).

Class 26 locomotives have always been uncommon north of Craigendoran, but to find one at Mallaig is rare indeed. No. 26034 was recorded for posterity on 26th May 1976, as it prepared to depart with the 14.05.
(Brian Morrison)

Above: In the late 1960s, an attempt was made to establish the re-engined North British Locomotive Co. Type 2s on the West Highland lines. They failed to oust the Sulzers and were relegated to secondary duties, before becoming extinct at the end of 1972. On 17th April 1968, No. D6129 awaits departure from Mallaig.
(W.S. Sellar)

Left: Three views of Mallaig station, charting the decline (and fall) of the overall roof. In the top picture, the canopy is very much intact as Class K1 No. 62012 indulges in a spot of shunting, on 21st July 1958. The centre picture, taken in June 1977, shows the structure being demolished. The bottom view dates from September 1983. A new booking office has been constructed and the main building roof has obviously been re-slated, as the skylight window visible in the 1977 shot has disappeared.
(Top: W.A.C. Smith)

Top right: For many years, railtours have been a major source of income for the Scottish Railway Preservation Society. These originate from locations throughout Scotland and Mallaig has always been a favourite destination. It became something of a tradition for an SRPS railtour to visit Mallaig on the first Saturday in August and it therefore comes as no surprise to find No. 27027 shunting the stock which had carried excursionists from Falkirk, on 2nd August 1975. They appear to have travelled in a mixture of BR stock and vehicles from the society's collection, such as the Caledonian Railway coach immediately behind the locomotive. Had it been required, this particular Class 27 would not have been able to supply train heat, as it was one of the batch built without a boiler.
(W.S. Sellar)

Above: Under the canopy at Mallaig sits No. 27019 on 1st July 1974, having arrived with the morning train from Fort William. These locomotives first worked the Extension in 1961 and officially replaced steam in 1962.
(John Goss)

Above: Class K2 2-6-0 No. 61764 *Loch Arkaig* relaxes outside Mallaig shed on 22nd July 1959. This was the last named Class K2 left in traffic, spending its twilight days on mundane duties around Glasgow before withdrawal in August 1961.
(Gavin Morrison)

Below: Mallaig in September 1983, with Class 37 No. 37051 idling away the time before departing on the 12.25 to Fort William. A road now runs through the site of the roofless, former engine shed, on the left of the picture, and the screen wall alongside the station has also gone.

The return of trainload fish

After an absence of more than 20 years, trainload fish traffic reappeared on the Mallaig Extension in March 1987 with a trial movement of a consignment bound for Grimsby. An Icelandic vessel landed the fish at Mallaig on 6th March and it was taken south in eleven insulated Interfrigo wagons, which were worked as a separate train to Mallaig Junction Yard for attachment to the following day's 06.01 Speedlink service to Mossend. The fish was packed in palletised boxes, the total load, including ice and packing, being almost 200 tonnes. The operation was the result of several months of planning by Icescot, a consortium of Icelandic and Scottish businesses. It led to further similar consign-ments, until the traffic was suspended in mid-summer, due to circumstances at the Iceland end. As a result 15 of the Interfrigo vans were stored at Mallaig Junction Yard, Fort William.

Pictured above is No. 37425 *Sir Robert McAlpine/Concrete Bob* approaching Corpach Wharf crossing with seven empty Interfrigo vans from Mallaig on 23rd May 1987. The vans were being moved to Fort William in order to accommodate a steam-hauled special at Mallaig the following day.

Left: Close-up of the type of van used, pictured at Mallaig.

A day in the life of No. 37425

Above: Summer and winter, the Extension has latterly had four passenger trains each way per day. Frequently, anyone observing the day's traffic saw only two individual locomotives. Taking Summer 1987 timings, whatever powered the 10.05 from Fort William also worked the 12.20 from Mallaig, the 14.05 from Fort William and the 15.50 from Mallaig, continuing south on the 17.40 Fort William–Glasgow.

On 25th May 1987, this pattern was being operated by No. 37425 *Sir Robert McAlpine/Concrete Bob*, which on 14th October 1986 had one nameplate unveiled at Fort WIlliam *(Sir Robert McAlpine)* and the other on Glenfinnan Viaduct. This is the 10.05 train, photographed between Arisaig and Morar.

Right: Near the previous location, No. 37425 heads the 12.20 ex-Mallaig service.

Right: It is now 15.30 and No. 37425 is near the end of its second westward trip of the day as it powers the 14.05 from Fort William away from Morar. It has, however, a different set of coaches, these three being the Glasgow portion of the Euston sleeper train.

Below: Thirty minutes later, locomotive and stock are on the move again, this time east of Morar on the 15.50 ex-Mallaig. A different locomotive will operate the rest of the day's services, stabling overnight at Mallaig and working the next morning's 06.50 Mallaig–Fort William and 08.30 Fort William–Glasgow.

Observation saloons of the 1980s

Observation saloons were taken off the West Highland line in the early 1960s and it was not until 1980 that a replacement appeared on the Extension. This was saloon DE 902260, which features in the colour section of this book. However this vehicle, named *Lochaber* and renumbered Sc1999, was single-ended and could not be turned at Mallaig. The difficulty was overcome in 1983 with the arrival of a second saloon, which allowed an observation car to be positioned at each end of the train. Pictured above is No. 37190 approaching Fort William on 9th August 1983 with the 16.10 from Mallaig, which has No. 1998 *Loch Eil* next to the locomotive and *Lochaber* on the rear. Both saloons are in LNER beech brown livery. No. 1998 *Loch Eil* was formerly DE 900580, built in 1936 and for many years the Eastern Region Chief Engineer's saloon. It received its name at Glasgow Queen Street on 27th May 1983. The picture on the right shows its full-length glass panels at the viewing end, which, if nothing else, must have given passengers a better impression of the sleepers.

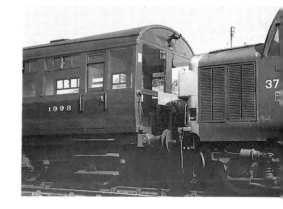

Right: The 1984 season's observation car was built in 1957 as a London Midland Region inspection saloon, latterly allocated to Dock Street Siding, Preston. It carried the number 999501, incorrectly prefixed by TODM. It had the advantage of windows at each end but observation saloons on the Extension fell out of favour with the operators and nothing was provided in 1985.

A revival in Steam

The return of steam to the Mallaig Extension in 1984, after an absence of more than 20 years, was a result of the efforts of the Fort William Area Business Group, a ScotRail initiative which gave local management much greater autonomy than had previously been enjoyed. Once all aspects of the proposal had been evaluated, a firm recommendation was passed to ScotRail House for formal approval. However, without the enthusiasm that existed at local level among management, staff and the tourist trade, this imaginative venture would have faltered.

The seeds were sown in August 1983, when two return diesel-hauled excursions between Fort William and Mallaig were run on four Sundays. The £3.50 return fare was aimed at getting holidaymakers out of their cars and an average of 200 passengers travelled on each return trip. Most of these people, a questionnaire revealed, were on a motoring holiday. This indicated that a market existed. In 1984, eleven diesel-hauled Sunday trips were scheduled – and steam was introduced as well.

Two ex-LMS Stanier Class 5 4-6-0 locomotives came north from Steamtown, Carnforth. (This class was once common south of Fort William but did not normally work the Mallaig route.) The Scottish Railway Preservation Society supplied its veteran North British Railway 0-6-0 No. 673 *Maude*. One of the Black Fives, LMS-liveried No. 5407, and *Maude* were towed from Eastfield depot in Glasgow to Fort William in a special train hauled by Class 37 diesel No. 37175. The trip, on 21st May, took nine hours and on arrival at Fort William *Maude* pulled the cavalcade, which included support vehicles and other stock, into the depot at Tom-na-faire. The other Black Five, No. 44767 *George Stephenson*, came up behind a diesel pilot some time later.

The honour of inaugurating the new age of steam on the Mallaig line went to No. 5407, which powered a press preview trip on 24th May. On Sunday 27th May, the same locomotive was in action on two specials organised by the Steam Locomotive Operators' Association. *Maude* should have been at the head of one of these trains but was temporarily sidelined by a broken eccentric strap. To the delight of enthusiasts, *Maude* set off next morning with three FOs and a Pullman brake. The day has gone down in West Highland railway history. In hindsight, too much was asked of *Maude*, which was struggling on the banks. It was decided to terminate at Arisaig, due to lack of time. *Maude* was held to await the arrival of the late-running 10.05 diesel service from Fort William then the NBR veteran began its return to the Fort.

Water had not been available at Arisaig and an unscheduled stop had to be made at Loch Dubh, between Beasdale and Lochailort, in order to replenish the tender with the aid of a portable pump, which someone of foresight had put aboard the train. It was a bad day for anything mechanical and more of the skill and patience which had carried *Maude* along was needed to get the pump to work. After stalling on the bank at Loch Eilt, *Maude* reached Glenfinnan and allowed the first public

---

The Locomotives

No. 44767 George Stephenson

London Midland & Scottish Railway Class 5 4-6-0 in BR livery. Built at Crewe in 1947 and the only one, of a class of 842, fitted with Stephenson outside link motion. This locomotive cost £13,226 to build, some £600 more than contemporary Walschaerts-motion engines. It originally had a double chimney and electric lighting, which were removed in 1953. Withdrawn in December 1967, and acquired for preservation, it was named *George Stephenson* at Shildon in 1975. It is owned by Mr Ian Storey and was based at Steamtown, Carnforth from 1981 until 1986 when it moved to the North Yorkshire Moors Railway. It has worked seasons 1984/85/86.

No. 5407

London Midland & Scottish Railway Class 5 4-6-0 in LMS livery. Built by Armstrong Whitworth at Newcastle-upon-Tyne in 1937. Withdrawn by BR from Lostock Hall shed in August 1968 at the end of steam. It is owned by Mr Paddy Smith and based at Steamtown, Carnforth. It has worked seasons 1984/85.

No. 673 Maude

North British Railway Class C 0-6-0 No. 673 *Maude*. (LNER and BR Class J36.) Built by Neilson & Co. of Glasgow in 1891 and rebuilt in 1915 with a larger boiler and enclosed cab. No. 673 was one of 25 similar locomotives sent to France in 1917 and, on its return, was named after General Sir Frederick Maude. Withdrawn as BR No. 65243 from Bathgate shed in 1966, it was bought by the Scottish Railway Preservation Society and extensively overhauled. *Maude* has appeared at countless railway events, including the 'Rocket 150' celebrations at Rainhill in 1980. Then based at the SRPS Falkirk depot, it operated on the Mallaig Extension only in 1984. It can now be found at the SRPS Bo'ness headquarters.

No. 44932

London Midland & Scottish Railway Class 5 4-6-0 in early BR black livery. Built at Horwich in 1945 and withdrawn in August 1968, following which its new owner had it restored in BR green livery. Sold about 1975, it ceased main line running around 1978. After extensive overhaul, it was steamed for the first time in more than six years in September 1985 and operated the Southport – Wigan shuttle that November. It is owned by Mrs Pat Parker and Mr Peter Wood and 1986 was its first West Highland season. It returned to the Midland Railway Centre at Butterley who share the locomotive with Steamtown, Carnforth in the ratio 3 : 1.

No. 5305 Alderman A.E. Draper

London Midland & Scottish Railway Class 5 4-6-0 in LMS mid-1940s black livery. Built by Armstrong Whitworth at Newcastle-upon-Tyne in 1936. Withdrawn August 1968 from Lostock Hall shed and sold for scrap to Albert Draper and Son of Hull. Restored by Humberside Locomotive Preservation Group and first steam tested on 12th June 1976. Named on 24th July 1984. Owned by Albert Draper and Son of Hull and maintained and operated by HLPG. Relieved No. 44932 towards the end of the 1986 season and worked the 1987 and 1988 seasons.

No. 2005

London & North Eastern Railway Class K1 2-6-0 No. 2005. Built in 1949 by the North British Locomotive Co. of Glasgow and run in from Eastfield depot until transfer to Heaton. Withdrawn in December 1967 and stored at Leeds Neville Hill for four years until moved to Thornaby for restoration by the North Eastern Locomotive Preservation Group. Officially entered service on the North Yorkshire Moors Railway on 8th June 1974. The locomotive is owned by NELPG and still based on the NYMR. Its first West Highland season was 1987 and it returned for 1988.

Above: The class of '84 – No. 5407, No. 44767 and *Maude* line up at Fort William depot.
(W.S. Sellar)

steam trip, which had been waiting for some time, to continue its way west.

The day's timetables were well and truly up in smoke, as were acres of heather all along the route, courtesy of *Maude*. Signalling cable had also been burned, causing a block failure which added to the complications. To be fair, the ground was tinder-dry, after a particularly long spell without rain. As it transpired, lineside fires were a major headache that first summer and insurance, damage claims and providing beaters accounted for seven per cent of the costs. The dry weather and the extensive vegetation which had developed in 22 years without the controlling influence of the steam locomotive, were contributory factors. There were other problems that first weekend, like a burst tank on a diesel locomotive which sprayed fuel over the approach to Glenfinnan. No wonder the following steam train needed

three attempts at the climb!

Maude was retired from active service and in July and August operated a Fort William–Glenfinnan and return Fridays-only excursion. This was entitled the "Glenfinnan Flyer", although it was suggested that, in view of *Maude's* fire-raising activities, the "Glenfinnan *Fryer*" would have been more apt! Maude *did* get to Mallaig, on 1st September, double-heading with No. 44767 *George Stephenson* on SLOA's "The Lochaber" railtour.

In 1984, steam trains ran on Wednesdays, Thursdays, and Sundays, with the two Black Fives sharing the duties. The stock used was elderly Mark One TSOs and BSOs and the adult return fare was £8. A total of 54 trips were operated, 26 more than originally intended, plus charters. More than 11,000 passengers were carried on the service trains and revenue, including long-distance fares paid by steam run

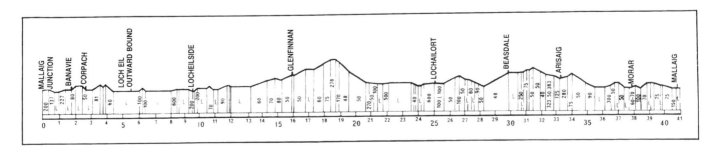

passengers, came to £120,000, of which costs totalled just over half. Steam boosted revenue on the Mallaig line generally by 45 per cent. It must be remembered that steam has to make a profit, as it cannot be financed from the Public Services Obligation grant and therefore comes under the InterCity sector, which requires to be commercial.

In the 1985 season, public steam running was stepped up to five days per week – Mondays, Tuesdays, Wednesdays, Thursdays and on Sundays, when there were two return trips. A major change was the advent of a dedicated set of coaches. These were refurbished Mark One vehicles, painted apple green and cream, separated by a thin black stripe; a livery based on the LNER Tourist stock of 1933. Much interest was also shown in the historic vehicles of the "Royal Scotsman" private luxury train, which included in its itinerary a steam-hauled return trip to Mallaig on Friday mornings.

The same two Black Fives were employed, except that when No. 5407 arrived on 4th July it was facing in the opposite direction, i.e. chimney leading from Mallaig. This opened up a whole new range of photographic possibilities – for all of 2½ weeks! That was No. 5407's total period of operating "about face" for on 7th August it was towed to Glasgow behind No. 37022, turned on the Cowlairs triangle and hauled back north by No. 37263 the following day.

The problem had been that No. 5407 would only partially fit over the inspection pit at Fort William depot. Some drivers also expressed reservations about tackling Beasdale Bank tender-first, as the sanders would be less effective.

The 1985 season surpassed the previous year, with more than 13,000 passengers travelling on steam runs. On several occasions, the 360-seat train was filled to capacity.

In 1986, No.44767 *George Stephenson* came back for its third spell, joined by a new stablemate in the shape of another Black Five, No. 44932, which had recently undergone a major overhaul. The apple green and cream steam set of coaches was again employed. Running days were reduced to four, dropping Wednesdays, with only one

Above: A 1988 innovation was the use of an ETHEL unit on some trains, in order to provide heating, chiefly at the start of the steam season. The former Class 25 locomotive, in InterCity livery, can be seen behind K1 No. 2005 in this 20th March 1988 view of the "West Highlander" excursion crossing over the main road near Beasdale. A total of 19 "West Highlanders" operated in 1988, with the fare for the three-day trip from St Pancras ranging from £215 to £245.
(Douglas Hume)

train on Sundays. This, however, offered a three-hour stay in Mallaig. The fares were held at the 1985 level of £9 adult return. Extremely healthy loadings were experienced and on occasions would-be passengers had to be turned away. In August the Sunday train was increased to seven coaches, to meet the demand. Once again, the "Royal Scotsman" was steam-hauled to Mallaig, this time on Wednesdays.

It is significant that when No. 44767 *George Stephenson* finished its stint on the Mallaig Extension in August 1986, it made its way to Inverness. From there, it worked a special train to Helmsdale and back on 31st August, the purpose of which was to test Radio Electronic Token Block equipment on a steam locomotive, in preparation for the introduction of this form of technology on the West Highland lines.

One of the lessons which has emerged is that 4-6-0 locomotives in good mechanical condition, particularly as regards axleboxes, suffer excessive tyre wear on the trailing driving wheel flanges, due to the curves on the Mallaig Extension. In the absence of turntable facilities, it has been suggested that one solution would be to bring the locomotives south halfway through their stint, in order to turn them on the Cowlairs triangle in Glasgow. The inspection pit at Fort William depot would, however, require to be altered. It was precisely this problem which curtailed No. 44932's West Highland sojourn. It worked the last public trip, on 25th September, then handed over the outstanding charter and "Royal Scotsman" work to the Hull-based Black Five No. 5305 *Alderman A.E. Draper,* which had been hastily drafted north, arriving at Fort William on 24th September.

More than 15,000 passengers were carried in 1986, an increase of some 2,000 on the previous year. This heartening figure, which represented 85 per cent loadings, was achieved with 24 fewer trains.

Black Five No. 5305 made the trip north again for the 1987 workings, during which it gained an enviable reputation for its superb exterior and mechanical condition. It was joined by the North Eastern Locomotive Preservation Group's LNER Class K1 2-6-0 No. 2005, whose sister locomotives were found on the Mallaig line before dieselisation.

For the first time, public trains ran on six Saturdays during July and August. An InterCity/Pullman Rail joint venture

Steam Stock

Introduced 1985:
BSO: 9312
TSO: 4050 4243 4494 4610 4623 4643
Withdrawn at the end of the 1987 season.

Introduced 1987:
BCK: IC 21241C
TSO: IC3766C IC3767C IC4419C IC4435C IC4900C IC4911C IC4912C

brought the "West Highlander" land cruise to the Extension on several Sundays. This was a three-day tour beginning and ending at St Pancras, which included steam haulage between Fort William and Mallaig in its itinerary. On Wednesdays, the "Royal Scotsman" could once again be found on the same route.

The upward trend in passenger figures continued, with over 16,500 travelling in 1987. A notable feature of the season was that both locomotives were returned south at the head of passenger trains – the first use of steam between Fort William and Glasgow since 1963. On 17th October, No. 5305 headed a return railtour to Edinburgh, with a diesel pilot from Craigendoran to Cowlairs. The pattern was repeated on 14th November, when it was the turn of the K1. Both trains were, of course, fully booked weeks in advance.

The same two locomotives were back in action for the 1988 workings, paired when necessary with an ETHEL (Electric Train Heating Ex-Locomotive) unit, converted from a Class 25, as steam heating of coaching stock had been eliminated. Each steam locomotive also had to be fitted with RETB equipment.

Steam has been a winner on the Mallaig line. It has boosted both the railway's business and the economy of the area, by attracting visitors. Part of the success story must lie in the fact that this is such a self-contained operation. The necessary skills – in driving, firing and maintenance – are there to be handed down; many of the problems can be solved locally.

It is to be hoped that steam will continue to be a part of the Mallaig Extension for a long time to come.

Above: At 08.25 on 28th May 1984, the Scottish Railway Preservation Society's veteran 0-6-0 *Maude* makes its presence felt at the Fort William suburb of Inverlochy. The ex-North British Railway locomotive, then 93 years old, was heading for Mallaig with a SLOA special composed of three FOs and a Pullman brake, all fully loaded. SRPS engineers had just completed the repairs needed to get their charge back in action.

Maude's first trip

Right: Having gone only as far as Arisaig, No. 673 *Maude* and the SLOA excursion are seen crossing Loch nan Uamh Viaduct, on the return trip. It had been a difficult day for *Maude,* which found itself short of breath on several occasions and short of water at least once. It was fortunate that the train appeared when it did, for the burning heather behind the photographer was becoming uncomfortably close!

Right: Behind time but battling bravely, *Maude* sets the camera shutters clicking as it continues its way west on its inaugural trip. However, the worst is yet to come, for Beasdale Bank lies ahead.

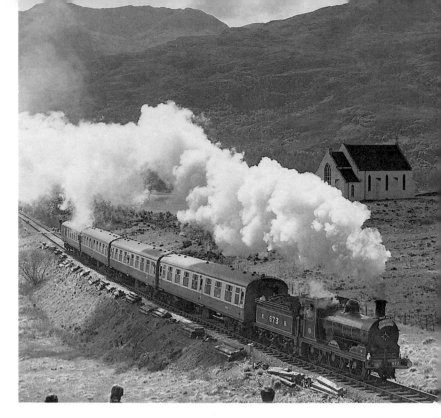

Below: Burning a mixture of Polish coal and Airth opencast, *Maude* tops the summit of the line west of Glenfinnan and prepares to glide down the Mhuidhe and wind round Loch Eilt. On the return trip, the equivalent climb to the summit overcame the veteran locomotive. This was the only time in the course of the day that *Maude* stalled, although speed had been down to a crawl on several occasions.
(John Hunt)

Right: Maude did not make a second solo attempt at reaching Mallaig in 1984 but it *did* get to the Extension's western terminus by partnering No. 44767 *George Stephenson* on SLOA's "The Lochaber" railtour. The date was 1st September, another of those days on which the weather ensured that lineside fires were unlikely, and the duo are seen west of Lochailort. A highlight of this trip was the fact that it left Mallaig Junction Yard *twice.* On the first attempt, it got as far as Banavie before returning to the junction to allow a diesel to go to the assistance of the 10.05 to Mallaig, whose locomotive had failed at Glenfinnan.
(Douglas Hume)

Maude
gets to
Mallaig

Below: A wisp of steam drifts from *Maude's* safety valves as "The Lochaber" crosses the Lochy Viaduct near Fort William on the return from Mallaig.

Above: The two-coach load of the "Glenfinnan Flyer" was more in keeping with *Maude's* capabilities. In front of an appreciative audience of photographers No. 673 tackles the climb from Glenfinnan Viaduct to the station in July 1984. *(Brian Dobbs)*

The Glenfinnan Flyer

Left: Maude sets a shining example of cleanliness as it simmers in the sunshine at Glenfinnan station on 20th July 1984. The semaphore signals have gone but *Maude* is, fortunately, still around. *(Brian Dobbs)*

Above: The cloudless sky and blue and grey stock in this 25th July 1984 shot of No. 44767 *George Stephenson* tackling Beasdale Bank evoke memories of the exciting days of the first year of steam specials.
(John Cooper-Smith)

Above: Arisaig signal box, like others on the Extension, was to the design of the Railway Signal Co. Passengers on the train alongside had ample time to appreciate its finer points, for their train – the already-late 12.20 from Mallaig, behind No. 37026 *Loch Awe* – was held at Arisaig for a further $2\frac{3}{4}$ hours on 28th May 1984, awaiting the first public steam train.

Top right: When No. 5407 appeared on the Sunday service on 19th August 1984, it had acquired a West Highland terrier motif on its cabside. The locomotive and train are pictured leaving Morar, on the outward leg.

Left: The long-awaited first public steam excursion from Fort William to Mallaig arrives at Arisaig, behind No. 5407, at 15.55 on 28th May 1984. Three minutes later, the delayed 12.20 ex-Mallaig got under way. Its booked departure time? – 12.42. Meanwhile, the passengers had made many new friends and the village shop had done very well, thank you!

Mindful of the fact that his passengers will be having lunch, the driver of No. 44767 *George Stephenson* takes it easy along by Loch Eil with the Mallaig – Fort William "Royal Scotsman" working of 21st May 1986.

Left: Evidence of sleeper replacement litters the lineside as No. 5305 climbs from Kinlocheil to Glenfinnan with the "Royal Scotsman" on 17th June 1987.

Right: Nostalgia is made of this – the locomotive, stock livery, and location are all pure LNER. This is the K1 at the east end of Loch Dubh on 24th August 1987, back in action after a boiler tube failure two days earlier.

Below: The jagged outline of Rhum and the distinctive shape of Eigg form the background to this shot of No. 5305 coasting down from Kinloid on 25th May 1987 with the first public steam trip of the season.

Above: The K1, disguised as No. 3445 *MacCailin Mor,* takes the seven-coach 11.05 from Fort William past Fassfearn on Sunday 30th August 1987.

Left: On 20th May 1987, No. 37402 *Oor Wullie* propels the Fort William tool van past Corpach, heading for the paper mill where the works shunter has derailed. The ''pepper pot'' canal lighthouse in the foreground dates from 1913.

Top right: The short length of 1 in 45/50 gradient, taking the line westward through a cleft in the hillside from Glenfinnan Viaduct to the station, usually has the locomotive working hard. On 31st May 1985, No. 44767 *George Stephenson,* at the head of the ''Royal Scotsman'', was no exception.

Bottom right: No. 44767 *George Stephenson* and the 11.05 Fort William – Mallaig are perfectly framed by a convenient tree near Locheilside, on 26th May 1985.

Left: Steam, sun and . . . snow! What a combination. No. 44767 *George Stephenson* powers a private charter away from Arisaig on 5th April 1986. *(Douglas Hodgins)*

Below: History, they say, begins yesterday. The once-familiar silhouette of a Class 37 crossing Lochy Viaduct with the late-evening Fort William – Mallaig service became merely a memory when the 'Sprinter' dmus invaded the West Highland lines in 1989.

Right: *Maude* and the 14.55 Glenfinnan–Fort William, pictured east of the Glenfinnan Viaduct on 13th July 1984, the first day of the ''Glenfinnan Flyer'' operation. The fares were £5.50 return; £3.50 single.
(Douglas Hume)

TO GLENFINNAN
by ''The Glenfinnan Flyer'' on.
Fridays, 13 July to 3 August
see the monument marking the spot where Bonnie Prince Charlie raised his standard in 1745 and visit the National Trust for Scotland Visitor Centre.

Left: On 20th July 1984, *Maude* departs from Glenfinnan with the 14.55 return to Fort William. The timings for the ''Glenfinnan Flyer'' were: Fort William depart 11.10, Glenfinnan arrive 11.54: Glenfinnan depart 14.55, Fort William arrive 15.30.
(Douglas Hume)

No. 44767

Right: The nameplate of No. 44767 *George Stephenson,* ceremonially named at Shildon on 25th August 1975, during the celebrations of the 150th anniversary of the Stockton & Darlington Railway.

Above: There is still snow on the hills around Glenfinnan on 22nd May 1986 as No. 44767 lifts the first public steam trip of the season up to the station. In 1986, *George Stephenson* arrived at Fort William on 24th March, having been towed up by No. 37406 on the path of the 09.52 Mossend–Corpach Speedlink train. It left, behind a diesel pilot, on 23rd August.

Right: Beasdale Bank begins after the tunnel at Loch nan Uamh Viaduct. It is a formidable climb and No. 44767 is pictured about to tackle it, on 25th June 1985. It was traditional on the West Highland Railway that all trains carried express headlamp codes, a practice which persisted throughout the decades to the steam trains of today. *(John Cooper-Smith)*

Bottom left: The classic location at Loch Eilt finds No. 44767 heading for Mallaig in July 1984. *(Brian Dobbs)*

Above: The 1 in 48 of Beasdale Bank levels off for about half-a-mile on reaching Beasdale station. No. 44767 can therefore grab a respite before climbing for a mile to the next summit, after which it is downhill to Arisaig. This is the 11.05 from Fort William on 4th August 1986, about to cross over the main road just west of Beasdale.

Left: SLOA's "West Highlander" railtour of 1st/2nd June 1985 involved a steam trip to Mallaig on the second day, using the normal steam set. It was worked by No. 44767 which is pictured crossing Keppoch Moss near Kinloid on the outward leg.
(Douglas Hume)

Top right: Near Kinlocheil, No. 44767's safety valves obligingly lift as the locomotive approaches with the 11.05 from Fort William on 4th August 1986. The boiler, incidentally, is the locomotive's fourth.

Above: The flat stretch of line around Keppoch Moss is left behind as No. 44767 opens up for the climb towards Arisaig with the 13.35 from Mallaig on 21st May 1985. This was one of the earliest outings for this steam set.

Left: Company travel buyers and other VIPs were the guests of the InterCity sector on this opulent train which traversed the Extension's metals on 2nd October 1984. It was made up of a BFK, an RKB, a Mark One FO and a Pullman saloon and Hadrian Bar car belonging to Pullman Rail. It was diesel-hauled from Glasgow Queen Street, the guests from London having travelled up overnight on the inaugural run of the "Starlight Express" Euston–Glasgow seating/sleeper train. No. 44767 took over at Fort William for the run to Mallaig and the ensemble is pictured approaching Glenfinnan. On the return, it had to cross the 16.05 from Fort William at Glenfinnan, *and* allow the 15.50 from Mallaig to overtake it – all three trains being in the vicinity of the station loops at the same time!

Above: The last three coaches betray the fact that this does not date from the days of BR steam. It is, in fact, an SRPS Edinburgh–Mallaig excursion on 2nd August 1986 which included three maroon-liveried vehicles owned by the society. The location is Loch Eil; the locomotive No. 44767.

Right: In the early days of the steam revival on the Extension, only five coaches were employed and this is the load behind the tender of No. 44767 as it leads the 13.15 from Fort William through the curves west of Glenfinnan on 22nd July 1984.

Bottom left: It is a clear road to Banavie for No. 44767 as it sprints past Mallaig Junction Yard in July 1984. When this locomotive was built in 1947, it was reckoned to have a standard life of 40 years. It should exceed that by a considerable margin!
(Brian Dobbs)

Above: One of the two SLOA specials of Sunday 27th May 1984 bowls along west of Kinlocheil, behind No. 5407. The track at this stretch is level for just over a mile but soon becomes a 1 in 60 climb towards Glenfinnan Viaduct. Of the 842 Black Fives, only 748 ever carried LMS numbers; the other 94 wore BR numbers from new.
(L.A. Nixon)

Right: A telephoto lens dramatically condenses the perspective as No. 5407 and the 13.35 from Mallaig get a clear road to Mallaig Junction on 18th July 1985. The trackwork on the right leads into the depot at Tom-na-faire.
(Brian Dobbs)

No. 5407

Top right: No. 5407 glides towards Banavie with the 15.15 from Fort William on Sunday 19th August 1984. Three days later, the locomotive left the West Highland for Edinburgh, to work a Festival Flyer special on 23rd August. Unfortunately, it sustained axlebox damage as it ran light between Glasgow and Edinburgh and the Festival Flyers of 23rd and 31st August had to be cancelled.

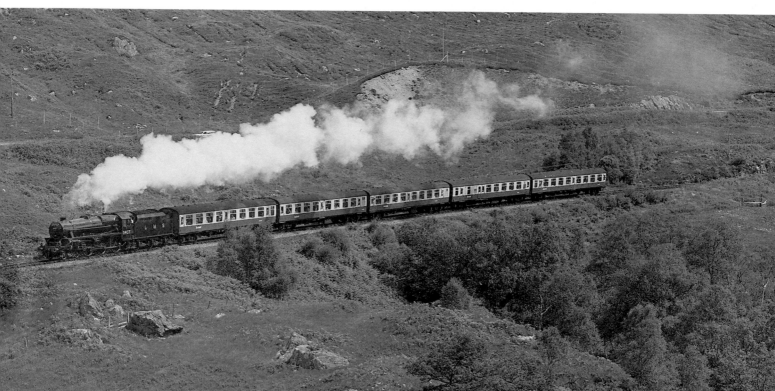

Paddy Smith's No. 5407 makes a stirring sight west of Glenfinnan with the 11.10 service from Fort William on 4th July 1984.
(Douglas Hume)

No. 5407 blasts up Beasdale Bank with the 15.15 from Fort William on Sunday 12th August 1984. This was booked into Mallaig at 16.56, with the return working leaving at 17.45 and arriving back in Fort William at 19.22.

Above: Loch nan Uamh Viaduct, photographed from the shore of the loch, with No. 5407 heading back to Fort William with the Sunday train of 12th August 1984. There was speculation in 1984 about a turntable being installed at Mallaig to avoid tender first running such as this, but nothing came of it.

Right: One of the SLOA specials of 27th May 1984 leaves Arisaig behind No. 5407.
(John Cooper-Smith)

No. 5407's change of direction

Above: On 19th July 1985, during the all-too-brief period when it ran chimney first from Mallaig, No. 5407 was photographed shortly after leaving for Fort William.
(Brian Dobbs)

Right: Having burst out of the westernmost tunnel at the end of Loch Eilt, No. 5407 and the 13.35 from Mallaig of 25th July 1985 are about to plunge into the second tunnel, above which the photographer is standing.
(John Cooper-Smith)

Above: In the 1985 season, two steam trips operated each way on Sundays. This is the second return journey – the 18.00 from Mallaig – on 14th July, with No. 5407 accelerating away from Glenfinnan Viaduct.

Left: On the same day, No. 5407 was captured at Loch Dubh, working the 13.35 from Mallaig.
(Douglas Hume)

Right: The 13.35 from Mallaig crossing Loch nan Uamh Viaduct on 25th July. Shots like this should make everyone grateful for No. 5407's about face, however brief it may have been.
(John Cooper-Smith)

Right: The fireman on No. 44932 seems determined to match the exhaust smoke to the colour of the locomotive on the climb to Glenfinnan Viaduct with the 11.05 from Fort William on 13th July 1986. (Perhaps it is just as well No. 44932 is no longer painted green!)

No. 44932

Below: No. 44932 glides around the curve and past the site of the long-gone Lochailort 'up' distant signal with the 11.05 Fort William – Mallaig on 14th July 1986. Some serious toiling is just about to to begin.

Above: No. 44932 near Locheilside with a westbound train in July 1986. The locomotive carries a shedcode plate reading 11A, which was Carnforth until 20th April 1958 when Carnforth was re-coded 24L and 11A became Barrow. On 9th September 1963, Carnforth was changed to 10A.

Right: The early BR livery carried by No. 44932 consisted of lined black, with the legend *British Railways* on the tender and no crest. This is clearly illustrated as the Black Five and the 13.35 from Mallaig prepare to cross the River Ailort, at the point where it flows into Loch Eilt. A Black Five's tender holds 4,000 gallons of water and nine tonnes of coal, of which three tonnes are used in a round trip on the Extension.

Above: No. 44932 and the 11.05 Fort William – Mallaig of 25th September 1986 are reflected in the still waters of Loch Eilt. This was the last public steam trip of the 1986 season and also the last outing on the line for No. 44932, which had experienced excessive tyre wear and was replaced by the Humberside-based Black Five No. 5305 *Alderman A.E. Draper.* This locomotive arrived at Fort William on 24th September and handled the remaining "Royal Scotsman" and charter work.

Right: Evidently No. 44932 is not short of steam as it comes off the Glenfinnan Viaduct with the Mallaig-bound train on 10th August 1986. A short, sharp climb lies ahead of it before a respite at Glenfinnan station.
(W.A. Sharman)

Right: Black Five No. 5305 is named *Alderman A.E. Draper,* after the Hull scrap dealer who saved it from the cutting torch. Mr Draper was twice Mayor of Hedon, East Yorkshire, and the Hedon coat of arms is mounted above the nameplates. The naming ceremony took place at York station on 24th July 1984.

No. 5305

Above: The driver of No. 5305 is making full use of the steam sanders on 17th August 1987, as the locomotive struggles to find its feet on Beasdale Bank in rain which could only be described as monsoon-like.

Above: St. Mary's, Arisaig, may not immediately spring to mind as one of the world's most-photographed churches. But since the Steam Revival, it has moved several places up the league table! This 18th August 1987 shot is typical, with No. 5305 providing the impetus.

Left: With seven coaches hung on the tender drawhook, No. 5305 approaches Annat signal box on Sunday 23rd August 1987. The section for which the fireman is holding the token is Mallaig Junction – Annat, as the new signal box at Banavie was not a block post, unlike its predecessor.

Right: The Lochy Viaduct at Fort William is of the standard West Highland Railway design and differs from structures farther south only in that the decking is attached half way up the girders, and not on top of them. Difficulties in constructing this bridge delayed the opening of the Banavie branch until some nine months after the main railway. No. 5305 is pictured rumbling across in August 1987.

Across the Lochy Viaduct

Above: No. 5305 takes an excursion train over the River Lochy on 30th August 1987.

Above: The boats may be high and dry but things are still buoyant in the steam-hauled trains business as No. 5305 heads past Corpach with yet another busy "West Highlander" tour from London. The date is 6th September 1987.

Below: The livery carried by No. 5305 is that of the London Midland & Scottish Railway in the mid-1940s, although the locomotive dates from 1936. It was therefore more than 50 years old when photographed on the "West Highlander" near Glenfinnan in August 1987.

The K1

Above: At long last, LNER Class K1 2-6-0 No. 2005 arrived in Fort William on 15th June 1987, having been towed from Glasgow by No. 37408 *Loch Rannoch.* It did not venture onto the Mallaig line until 28th June and this is that first outing pictured at Banavie.

Right: The same train, photographed later that day on the gradients leading to the summit west of Glenfinnan. The Mallaig route was to give the K1 ample opportunity to demonstrate its hill-climbing abilities.

Above: According to the purists, excessive smoke effects are achieved only by inefficient firing or stage-management by photographers. Whatever the reason, performances such as this by the K1 at Mallaig Junction Yard on 30th June 1987 linger in the memory long after the smoke has dispersed.
(Brian Dobbs)

Top right: The hills are alive with the sound of (steam) music as No. 2005 pounds up the bank high above Loch nan Uamh with the 11.05 from Fort William on 1st September 1987. Lineside vegetation had recently been cut back at this location, thus improving it for photography. The headboard reads "The Flying Kipper", about which the least said the better.

Bottom right: No. 2005 pictured west of Lochailort, in charge of the original set of coaches dedicated to steam services. These carried the legends "West Highland" and "ScotRail" on the sides, unlike the second rake which arrived in July 1987 and which proclaimed only "West Highland Line".

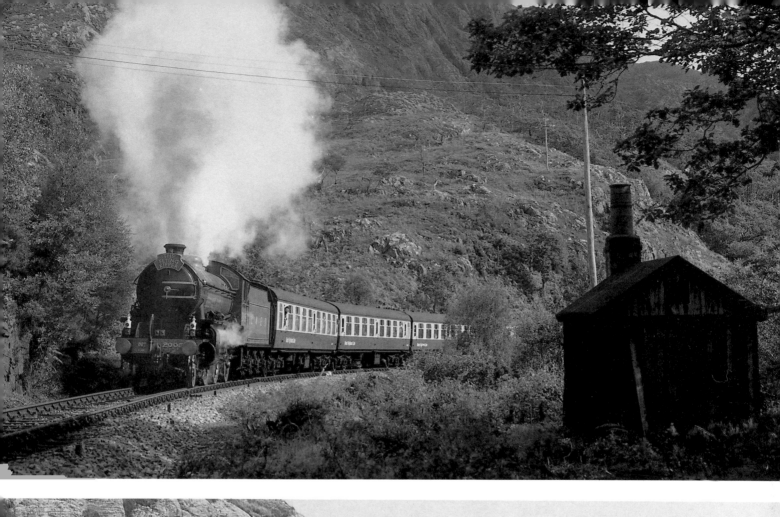

Right: The eastern end of Loch Eilt on 28th July 1987, with No. 2005 sprinting up towards the twin tunnels, and then the summit of the line, with a Fort William-bound train. The locomotives tender holds 5$^1/_2$ tonnes of coal and 3,500 gallons of water.

Below: LNER Class K1/1 2-6-0 No. 3445 *MacCailin Mor* pictured near Glenfinnan on 30th August 1987! Perhaps 1st April would have been a more appropriate date, for this is a little jest by the NELPG. For one day, No. 2005 was disguised as *MacCailin Mor* – the prototype for the Class K1 – by means of stick-on numbers and a remarkably authentic-looking wooden nameplate, on one side only. (Viewed from the other side, it was still No. 2005). In this condition, it worked the day's service trains and, on return to Fort William depot, reverted to its true identity.

The Royal Scotsman

In 1985, the Great Scottish & Western Railway Co. began operating its "Royal Scotsman" luxury touring train, which carried a maximum of 28 passengers on three-day and six-day holidays along Scotland's scenic routes. The eight-vehicle train was made up of a service car, housing a generator, three sleeping cars, a state car (cabins with private bathrooms) and three day cars. These were:

The observation car (CR 41): Built in 1892 as a dining car for West Coast Joint Stock, it passed to the Caledonian Railway in 1905; became an inspection saloon in 1933 and in the 1960s was converted to an observation vehicle. At the same time the body was fitted to a 1927 chassis – its third!

The saloon car (GNR 807): Constructed in 1912 for the Great Northern Railway, it has a varnished teak exterior. Built as a family saloon, with sections for ladies and children, gentlemen and servants. Now used for dining and relaxing.

The dining car (LNWR 5159): Dates from 1891 when it was built for London – Manchester expresses on the London & North Western Railway. Became part of a house in the 1920s and restored to original condition in the 1980s, incorporating modern cooking facilities. The oldest operating dining car in the world.

The other vehicles were rebuilt from 1960's BR coaches and more than £1m was spent on restoring and converting the "Royal Scotsman" stock. A ninth coach – a crew sleeping car – was added in 1987.

The "Royal Scotsman" is usually hauled by a Class 37 diesel locomotive, except between Fort William and Mallaig, where steam takes over. In 1987, prices per person ranged from £1,090 for a three-day tour to £2,490 for six days in a state cabin, inclusive of everything except gratuities and insurance.

The stillness of an April morning in 1986 is broken by No. 44767 and the "Royal Scotsman" skirting the shore of Loch Eil.
(Douglas Hume)

Above: In May 1985, No. 44767 creeps round Loch Eilt with the "Royal Scotsman".
(Douglas Hume)

Below: On Wednesday 27th July 1988, K1 No. 2005 hauls the returning "Royal Scotsman" past Corpach. Two days earlier, unseasonal gales had lashed Scotland and the beached yacht was one of the many casualties. At one point it was feared the vessel's mast would foul the railway line and endanger trains.

Above: At 07.15 on 31st May 1985, Ian Storey's unique Black Five (fitted with Stephenson outside link motion) No. 44767 leaves a fine trail of smoke as it hustles the "Royal Scotsman" out of Fort William. On such a beautiful morning, who minds the early start?

Above: Some 25 minutes later, the same train was captured by the camera climbing from Kinlocheil to Glenfinnan Viaduct. Arrival in Mallaig was booked for 08.50.
(Douglas Hume)

Above: Passengers are treated to fleeting glimpses of Loch nan Uamh as the "Royal Scotsman" plunges in and out of the tunnels on Beasdale Bank. There are still 11½ miles ahead of No. 44932 and its prestigious train before Mallaig is reached. The date is 3rd September 1986 and immediately behind the locomotive are the three historic day coaches – observation car CR 41, the LNWR dining carriage and the GNR teak saloon.

Left: A reflection of gracious living – the "Royal Scotsman" on one of the causeways at Loch Eilt. On a fine day, a trip along the Extension must be worth every dollar!

Above: No doubt the passengers enjoying the luxury of the "Royal Scotsman" will be equally appreciative of the view down Loch Shiel afforded by Glenfinnan Viaduct. As they contemplate the monument commemorating the '45 Rebellion and Bonnie Prince Charlie, they might like to consider that there is only one Glenfinnan memorial to a man of vision – and that is the structure they are currently crossing.

Right: The Mallaig Extension is a line of contrasts. It can be sun-soaked and scenic, damp and defeating or, as in this case, moody and menacing. Like a spotlight, a shaft of sunshine pierces a September morning in 1987 and traps K1 No. 2005 and the "Royal Scotsman" as they approach Glenfinnan station. *(John Cooper-Smith)*

Above: On the sparkling morning of 20th May 1987, No. 5305 leads the "Royal Scotsman" across Loch nan Uamh Viaduct. Each arch has the standard Extension span of 50ft.

Right: Mallaig on 17th June 1987. Having arrived with the "Royal Scotsman", No. 5305 has taken water and is now running round its train, in preparation for departure at 10.55. Passengers have just under an hour at Mallaig.